The 100 Greatest
New Orleans
Creole Recipes

The 100 Greatest
New Orleans
Creole Recipes

ROY F. GUSTE, JR.

PELICAN PUBLISHING COMPANY
Gretna 1994

First published by W. W. Norton & Company, Inc., in New York
    and London, and by Penguin Books Canada Ltd., 1988

Published by arrangement with the author by
    Pelican Publishing Company, Inc., 1994

First Pelican edition, September 1994

*The word "Pelican" and the depiction of a pelican are trademarks
of Pelican Publishing Company, Inc., and are registered in the
U.S. Patent and Trademark Office.*

Library of Congress Cataloging-in-Publication Data

Guste, Roy F.
   [100 greatest dishes of Louisiana cookery]
   The 100 greatest New Orleans creole recipes / Roy F. Guste, Jr. —
1st Pelican ed.
      p.   cm.
   Originally published: The 100 greatest dishes of Louisiana
cookery. 1st ed. New York : Norton, c1988.
   Includes index.
   ISBN 1-56554-046-8
   1. Cookery, American—Louisiana style. 2. Cookery, Creole.
3. Cookery—Louisiana—New Orleans.   I. Title. II. Title: One
hundred greatest New Orleans creole recipes.
   TX715.2.L68G83 1994
   641.5'9763—dc20

94-20650
CIP

Manufactured in the United States of America
Published by Pelican Publishing Company, Inc.
1101 Monroe Street, Gretna, Louisiana 70053

To Mimi,
again and perhaps always.

Contents

The 100 Greatest
New Orleans
Creole Recipes

Introduction

Many writings on Louisiana cookery have lost that essential ingredient that makes the cuisine so very pure and original—its simplicity. Flavorful and complicated are not necessarily synonymous. You mustn't lose the beauty of the dishes by adding too many herbs and spices and some of those inexcusables: powdered onion, powdered garlic, (both of which taste of chemicals), store-bought, pre-mixed herb combinations. Louisiana cuisine is simple and relies in the end on very few specific tastes, not on a plethora of complicated combinations. What is the use of going through great pains to find the freshest fish available if your dish is marred by the chemical tastes in powdered and dried ingredients? And condiments belong on the table, not in your sauce. Even the most excellent products such as Worchestershire and Tabasco sauce belong on the dining table, not in the kitchen. They have no stability in a heated sauce—they either cook out too quickly or lay in the mixture with an unpleasant heaviness. Mincing a clove of garlic, chopping an onion, and learning the proper use of cayenne is easy enough that any cook can quickly learn these steps in a manner that soon becomes second nature.

Whenever possible I eliminated steps in the cooking processes. An extra pan to pre-brown, a useless pre-cooking or poaching, all gone. I have tested this entire book using only four saucepans and a skillet, and for utensils, a kitchen fork, a wooden spoon, a spatula, a small whisk and two knives—one paring, one chopping—and a chopping board. That's all you need. There is no need for choppers, blenders, mixers or food processors. I use these mechanisms regularly, but they are not necessary to produce the recipes in this book. So clear off your kitchen counter and get out your chopping knife and your cutting board and start *simple,* as cooking should be.

Are these the best recipes available for the dishes included here? No! The best recipes for the dishes included here will be developed by you in your own kitchen. The most important key to Louisiana cookery is that no two cooks prepare any single dish exactly the same way. We all have our own palates and our cooking will eventually reflect that individuality, and rightly so. So relax and cook.

Remember to read the entire piece on each dish. Important information is given throughout the story, the recipe, the variations, and the notes. Read all of it. I have striven to produce the most basic and uncomplicated recipe for each dish, but you will often find that a variation or some personal idea that I imparted strikes home and should be tried first. That's what makes cooks cooks: their individual tastes and ideas.

All of my ramblings on about the dishes and New Orleans and growing up and who did what and why is nothing more than personal indulgence, that I hope will hold some interest for you, and help you to understand the recipes and my feelings about them.

I have chosen recipes to present to you the dishes I feel are the most famous, the best, and the simplest of Louisiana cookery. There may be dishes that you feel should have been chosen over others. Unfortunately there are many, many dishes that are not here because I have limited myself to one hundred recipes. I have left some very obvious recipes out because I feel that they are more complicated and will be included in the next volume.

Next volume?

Yes, next volume! Of course there is no way that all of Louisiana cookery can be included in such limited a work as this, but through the years, as these works are developed, I hope to have documented the entirety of Louisiana cookery. So keep space on your shelf next to this book. You will need it.

Cocktails

The drink called the "cocktail" and the name itself are both said to have been born in New Orleans.

In 1793 there was an uprising of the natives of San Domingo and many of the wealthy French plantation owners fled for their lives making their way to New Orleans. One such refugee, Antoine Amedee Peychaud, arrived in the city with nothing but the clothes on his back and an education as an apothecary. He soon managed to open a small dispensary where he won popularity with a tonic for stomach disorders that he called "bitters."

These bitters were served in an egg cup or the french *coquetier,* and mixed with a little cognac. The cup was used for the proper measure and the cognac for flavor. Peychaud's bitters soon found their way into the many coffee houses in the city and the drink became known as the cocktail, an American mispronunciation of *coquetier.*

Stanley Clisby Arthur, in his work *Famous New Orleans Drinks and How to Mix 'Em* (1937), states that "Other and more fanciful legends have found circulation from time to time but here are the facts concerning the birth of the cocktail and how it received its inapposite name . . ." My story is drawn from his and from various anecdotes repeated to me through the years. Also John Mariani, in his *Dictionary of American Food and Drink* (1983), relates this story as one of the possible origins of the name *cocktail.*

SAZERAC

One of the first establishments in New Orleans serving cocktails was the Sazerac Coffee House on Exchange Alley. It was opened in 1859 be John B. Schiller who named the business after the Sazerac-de-Forge brand cognac that he served there.

Schiller's business flourished and he eventually sold it to his bookkeeper Thomas H. Handy in 1870. It was under Handy that the popular cocktail of bitters and cognac was transformed into a mixture including absinthe and substituting rye whiskey for the cognac. It was this drink that came to be known as the "Sazerac."

2 three-and-a-half ounce
    "old fashioned"
    cocktail glasses
½ cup crushed ice
1 teaspoon sugar
1 dash Peychaud Bitters
1 dash angostura bitters
1½ ounces rye whiskey
1 dash herbsaint liqueur or
    absinthe substitute
1 lemon twist

Pack a 3½ ounce old fashioned cocktail glass with crushed ice. Set aside. In a second glass blend the sugar with the Peychaud and angostura bitters and the rye whiskey until the sugar is dissolved. Add a cube of ice and stir to chill. Now discard the crushed ice from the first glass. Add a dash of herbsaint and twirl it around to coat the inside of the glass. Discard the ice cube from the other glass and pour its contents into this glass. Twist a lemon peel into the cocktail and serve.

VARIATIONS:

You can make an agreeable cocktail using bourbon or brandy in place of the rye whiskey.

Note:

The purists insist that after coating the glass with the herbsaint, that which settles to the bottom of the glass should be poured out.

The purists also feel that the lemon twist should be twisted over the cocktail but never dropped in.

RAMOS GIN FIZZ

The gin fizz is an old New Orleans favorite that existed for some time before Henry C. Ramos developed his own special recipe. In 1888 Ramos arrived in New Orleans and purchased the Imperial Cabinet Saloon, where he first served his version that grew so popular he moved his business to a larger location on Gravier Street.

The popularity of his Ramos Gin Fizz was such by 1915, that at Mardi Gras of that year there were 35 boys employed solely for the purpose of shaking the fizzes and still they could not keep up with the demand.

Ramos Gin Fizzes are a marvelous way to start off a Sunday brunch, or maybe just the thing to take the edge off the night before.

Pour all the ingredients into a cocktail shaker and shake vigorously for at least 3 minutes or until the mixture acquires a somewhat thickened consistency.

Strain into a tall cocktail glass and serve immediately.

1 egg white
1 ounce heavy cream
1 tablespoon powdered
     sugar
Juice of ½ lemon
Juice of ½ lime
4 drops orange flower water
1½ ounce gin
2 ounce soda water
½ cup crushed ice

VARIATIONS:

Some mixologists add 2 drops of vanilla extract. Milk or cream can be used in place of the heavy cream but the resulting texture will not be as thick. Sometimes this cocktail is dusted with ground nutmeg, but I prefer to reserve the nutmeg for the Brandy Milk Punch.

BRANDY MILK PUNCH

Brandy Milk Punch is a popular brunch drink served as a brunch aperitif. It also helps cure your ills from the night before.

2 teaspoons powdered sugar
2 drops vanilla extract
¾ cup milk or light cream
1½ ounces brandy
½ cup crushed ice
Freshly grated nutmeg

Put the sugar, vanilla extract, milk, and brandy in a cocktail shaker with ½ cup crushed ice. Shake briefly and strain into a highball glass. Dust the top with grated nutmeg. Makes 1 cocktail.

VARIATIONS:

Bourbon, rye, or blended whiskey make good punches.

MINT JULEP

The Mint Julep is the ultimate Southern summer cocktail. It's extremely refreshing and quickly gets one into the right mood for passing those hot, languid afternoons on the verandah.

Put the mint leaves in the bottom of a tall highball glass with the sugar. Using a spoon or muddler, crush the leaves in the sugar. Add the bourbon and fill with crushed ice. Garnish with a sprig of mint. Serve with a straw. Makes 1 cocktail.

6 mint leaves
2 teaspoons powdered sugar
2 ounces bourbon
Crushed ice
1 mint sprig

VARIATIONS:

You can use rye or blended whiskey in place of the bourbon.

NOTE:

The cocktail should be stirred long enough before serving for frost to form on the glass. The glass must be dry on the outside or the frost will not form.

Traditionally Mint Juleps were served in silver tumblers.

HURRICANE

Anyone who has not had a Hurricane at Pat O'Brien's has not been to New Orleans. The drink is a sort of fruit punch with citrus juice and lots of rum and is a must in starting your stay in New Orleans in the proper fashion.

A special glass was designed for the Hurricane, shaped like the glass windshade of a kerosene hurricane lamp.

The Hurricane packs such a wallop that unsuspecting imbibers may feel they are spinning in the storm of the same name.

1 ounce lemon juice
4 ounces dark rum
2 ounces red passion fruit
    cocktail mix
Crushed ice
Orange slice and
    maraschino cherry for
    garnish

Shake the lemon juice, rum and passion fruit cocktail mix together in a cocktail mixer and pour into a hurricane glass or tall ice tea glass packed with crushed ice. Garnish with the orange slice and maraschino cherry. Serve with tall straws. Makes 1 cocktail.

VARIATIONS:

Hawaiian Punch base can be used instead of the Red Passion Fruit Mix. They are almost identical.

More lemon can be used to cut the sweetness if you prefer.

NOTE:

This is the original recipe and is actually older than the one served at Pat O'Brien's.

Too many of these will give you the worst hangover in the history of mankind.

ABSINTHE FRAPPÉE

This is one of the numerous absinthe drinks that came out of Cayetano Ferrer's Absinthe Room of the early 1870s. That location still stands today as the Old Absinthe House on Bourbon Street. Absinthe was eventually banned because of the harmful nature of one of it's principle ingredients, *Artemisia absinthium,* more commonly called wormwood.

Since that time many absinthe substitutes have become quite popular. Herbsaint is a Louisiana version which takes its name from the Louisiana-French name for wormwood, *herbe sainte.*

Pack a tall highball glass with crushed ice and add the herbsaint and anisette. Fill with soda water. Put a teaspoon or ice-tea spoon into the glass and shake the ice with the spoon until a frost forms on the outside of the glass. Serve with a straw. Makes 1 cocktail.

1 cup crushed ice
1 ounce herbsaint or
     absinthe substitute
1 ounce anisette
Soda water

VARIATIONS:

A teaspoon of simple syrup can be added for additional sweetness. Some people add an eggwhite to the mixture and shake it before pouring it into the glass.

NOTE:

Absinthe substitutes are strongly flavored with anise and should be served only to those who like that particular taste.

In France some of the most popular toothpastes have an absinthe flavor.

OLD FASHIONED

The Old Fashioned cocktail has been popular in New Orleans for almost a century. It even has its own squat glass called the "old fashioned" glass.

1 teaspoon powdered sugar
1½ ounce bourbon
1 dash angostura Bitters
Maraschino cherry
Orange slice

Put the sugar, bourbon and bitters in an old fashioned glass and stir until the sugar is dissolved. Fill the glass with ice cubes and garnish with a maraschino cherry and a slice of orange. Makes 1 cocktail.

VARIATIONS:

Rye or blended whiskey may be used instead of bourbon.

NOTE:

Even though this cocktail has lost much of its general popularity in the city, there is a large group of New Orleanians who still prefer it over other cocktails.

ANTOINE'S SMILE

This cocktail, invented at Antoine's, is a sort of high rent "sour." It is good natured and packs a punch.

Dampen the rim of a champagne glass and dip it in a dish of granulated sugar. Set the glass aside. Shake the calvados, lemon juice, sugar, and grenadine together in a cocktail shaker with ½ cup crushed ice and strain into the prepared glass. Makes 1 cocktail.

Granulated sugar
1 ½ ounce calvados or apple
    brandy
½ ounce lemon juice
1 teaspoon powdered sugar
Dash grenadine syrup
½ cup crushed ice

VARIATIONS:

Your preference of liquor in place of the brandy will do.

CAFÉ BRÛLOT
À LA DIABOLIQUE

There is no more perfect end to a grand style New Orleans dinner than Café Brûlot. That rich combination of brandy, spices, and hot, dark coffee is just what you need to give you that last burst of energy to end the evening.

Café Brûlot was created by my great grandfather, Jules Alciatore for his patrons at Antoine's. He designed special cups and even the decorative suspended copper bowl in which to blend and flame the mixture.

Café Brûlot is available at most of the old restaurants and the special cups and bowl can be bought at the finest stores in the city.

6 ounces brandy
Peel of 1 lemon
2 sticks cinnamon
8 whole cloves
1½ tablespoons sugar
4 cups strong, hot, black
    coffee

In a fireproof bowl, over an open flame, or stove, combine the brandy, lemon peel, cinnamon sticks, cloves and sugar. As the mixture heats, ignite carefully with a match. Use a ladle to stir the liquid for about 2 minutes. Pour hot coffee into the flaming brandy and ladle into demitasse cups or serve a half cup in regular coffee cups. Serves 6.

VARIATIONS:

If you prefer more sweetness add more sugar. The addition of 2 ounces of Grand Marnier or orange curaçao to the bowl before heating is quite good.

Appetizers

OYSTERS ROCKEFELLER

In 1899 my great-grandfather, Jules Alciatore, created Oysters Rockefeller at Antoine's. Jules was the second generation proprietor; his father was Antoine himself.

At the time, there was a shortage of snails from France but an abundance of oysters in Louisiana. Oysters seemed to Jules the obvious replacement for escargot. But cooked oysters? That had not yet been done except perhaps in soups. Jules thought that if snails could be cooked and served in their shells, why not oysters? And so the idea began. He decided to bake oysters on the half shell, using a bed of rock salt to keep them hot. For the sauce he decided to make use of the table relishes—green onions, celery, parsley—that were often returned untouched to the kitchen and discarded. The result was a green sauce that required an equally elegant name. Oysters Rockefeller was a perfect name for a dish of such wealth of flavor, and the name would be remembered and identified with Antoine's for years to come.

Oysters Rockefeller was born. Jules not only created the sauce, but he opened up a whole new genre of cooking by baking an oyster on the half-shell with sauce.

3 dozen shelled raw oysters
    in their liquor
½ teaspoon salt
1 lemon, juiced

½ stick butter
4 tablespoons flour
2 bunches parsley, all stems
    removed, finely minced
2 bunches green onions,
    finely minced
8 ribs celery, all strings
    removed, finely minced
4 tablespoons tomato paste
1½ tablespoons sugar
1 tablespoon vinegar
1 tablespoon salt, or to
    taste
1 teaspoon ground white
    pepper
½ teaspoon cayenne
½ cup bread crumbs

6 small ovenproof baking
    dishes

Prepare the oysters.

Poach the oysters in their own liquor with the ½ teaspoon salt and the juice from 1 lemon for 1 minute or just until their edges barely begin to curl. Do not boil. Strain the oysters, reserving 1 cup of their liquid, and set aside.

Make the Rockefeller Sauce.

Melt the butter in a heavy saucepan. Add the flour and cook for 2 minutes without coloring. Blend in the 1 cup reserved oyster poaching liquid. Blend in the minced parsley, green onion and celery. Add the tomato paste, sugar, vinegar, salt, pepper and cayenne. Simmer very, very slowly for 1 hour and 15 minutes. Add the bread crumbs and adjust seasonings according to taste.

Assemble the dish.

Arrange the oysters in individual oven proof dishes, 6 oysters per serving, and spoon over the Rockefeller sauce. Bake in a preheated 400 degree oven for 12 minutes or until the sauce is bubbly and beginning to brown. Serves 6.

VARIATIONS:

Most recipes call for spinach, though it is not employed in the original recipe. Some cooks like the sauce to be very green and use green food coloring while others add Worcestershire and hot pepper sauce or Herbsaint or Pernod. The final touches will always depend on your own palate.

I have seen this sauce successfully employed as a sauce served over fried trout, as a sauce for pasta, and even as the base for a soufflée. I have never had Oysters Rockefeller done as well as it is done in the location of its origin, Antoine's.

I have simplified assembly and baking of the recipe by calling for the use of ovenproof dishes. Normally in restaurants the oysters would be baked on the half-shell, in pie pans filled with rock salt.

NOTES:

The notes here are of the utmost importance if you want the sauce to turn out correctly. You must be absolutely positive that you scrape all the strings from the celery stalks. If you don't, you will never get the proper texture, there will always be stringy bits in the sauce no matter how finely you chop. Remove all stems from the parsley or you will get a bitterness that you will not be able to eliminate.

When I say to simmer *very, very slowly,* I mean it. Some of the best chefs in New Orleans scorch this sauce regularly because it takes a long time on a low fire with regular stirring and a good cover on the pot. Don't let it blop and bubble. Don't try to rush it. Absolutely all of the raw green taste of the vegetables needs to be cooked out in order for the sauce to acquire the rich and marvelous taste for which it is so justly famous. This is one of the reasons that this sauce is so difficult to prepare properly.

This is not the actual used at Antoine's, but is one I have specifically devised for this book to produce the authentic taste of the original with the least amount of ingredients and effort. It is the recipe I use when I prepare Oysters Rockefeller at home.

SHRIMP REMOULADE

Shrimp Remoulade is one of the most basic dishes of Louisiana cookery, but it is truly a difficult dish to explain. There are too many remoulades! The classic French remoulade is a mayonnaise-base sauce, whereas a Creole remoulade is a Creole mustard-base sauce. There are many who opt to use ketchup in the Creole remoulade with the mustard. Neither is incorrect, but the Creole mustard sauce seems to be the original Louisiana remoulade.

1 cup light olive oil
⅓ cup vinegar
1 teaspoon salt
½ teaspoon cayenne
1 tablespoon paprika
¾ cup Creole mustard
½ bunch minced green
    onions
2 tablespoons minced
    parsley
1 rib celery, minced
3½ quarts water
4 tablespoons salt
1 tablespoon cayenne
4 bay leaves
12 peppercorns
1 sliced lemon
2 pounds medium shrimp
6 lettuce leaves
3 lemons, cut into wedges

Whisk the olive oil, vinegar, salt, cayenne and paprika together in a bowl. Blend in the Creole mustard, green onions, parsley and celery. Cover and chill.

Boil the shrimp. Put the water in a pot with the salt, cayenne, bay leaves, peppercorns and sliced lemon. Bring to a boil. Add the shrimp and bring back to a boil. Turn off the heat immediately and let the shrimp soak for 5 minutes, then remove them from the water. When the shrimp are cool, peel them. Put the shrimp in a bowl and blend with the remoulade sauce. Cover and chill for a few hours.

Spoon the Shrimp Remoulade into the lettuce leaves and garnish with lemon wedges. Serves 6.

VARIATIONS:

A hot sauce can be added for additional spiciness, as can horseradish. The juice of half a lemon in the sauce is also a nice addition. Some prefer to serve the Shrimp Remoulade with quartered lemons for squeezing at the table.

Both crabmeat and crayfish make lovely substitutions for the shrimp.

NOTE:

Allowing the shrimp to chill in the sauce improves the taste absorption of the shrimp. They could be chilled overnight if properly covered and protected from the air.

This recipe is one I devised to resemble the remoulade served at Arnaud's Restaurant where it is called "Shrimp Arnaud." That preparation is to me the most authentic Creole Remoulade.

CRABMEAT RAVIGOTE

This lovely little appetizer was concocted with lightness and zip in mind. It should be served very cold before the entrée or as a light meal in itself. Its name comes from the French *ravigoter* meaning to invigorate or enliven. And so it does enliven the palate.

1 whole egg
½ teaspoon salt
¼ teaspoon white pepper
Pinch cayenne
1 cup peanut oil
2 tablespoons lemon juice
1½ tablespoons each of
    minced bell pepper,
    green onion, pimento,
    and anchovy
1½ pound fresh lump
    crabmeat
6 nice lettuce leaves,
    washed

Make the sauce (mayonnaise):

Beat the egg together with the salt, white pepper, and cayenne. While beating, slowly pour the oil in a thin stream into the mixture until it has all been incorporated. Beat in the lemon juice. Blend in the minced bell pepper, green onion, pimento and anchovy. Chill. Makes 1 cup.

Assemble the dish:

Carefully fold the sauce into the crabmeat. Don't work it too much because you don't want to break up the lump crabmeat. Adjust seasoning per taste. Chill.

When ready to serve, spoon the Crabmeat Ravigote onto the lettuce leaves and serve on cold salad plates. Serves 6.

VARIATIONS:

As in the case of many of our dishes, we can substitute boiled shrimp or crayfish or even a combination of shrimp, crayfish, and crab. Now that's an exciting little treat for even the most jaded gourmets. I personally serve this dish whenever I have several appetizers for my guests to taste.

NOTE:

Cut back on the mayonnaise if there is too much for you.

This dish should be quite cold. It is a favorite summertime luncheon dish for many and light enough to please the dieters.

CRAYFISH CARDINAL

This preparation takes on a reddish or "cardinal" color from the tomato paste used in its preparation. Again, simplicity is the key here along with quality and freshness of ingredients.

Crayfish do have a distinct taste and therefore lend themselves to this combination of flavors.

Melt ½ stick butter in a small skillet and fry the French bread rounds to make the croutons. Set aside.

Melt the 4 tablespoons of butter and blend in the flour. Cook together without coloring for 2 minutes. Add the green onions, the wine, and the milk and bring to a simmer. Add the tomato paste, salt, ground white pepper, and cayenne. Add the crayfish tails and simmer for 10 minutes. Adjust seasoning.

Spoon the Crayfish Cardinal into small bowls and serve garnished with the croutons for dipping. Serves 6.

½ stick butter
12 ½ inch thick rounds of
     French bread

4 tablespoons butter
3 tablespoons flour
½ bunch green onions,
     chopped
¼ cup white wine
1¼ cup milk
1 tablespoon tomato paste
2 teaspoons salt
½ teaspoon ground white
     pepper
¼ teaspoon cayenne
1½ pounds crayfish tails

VARIATIONS:

Shrimp is the most obvious. Oysters and crabmeat in this sauce make a nice dish. Crabmeat alone is also excellent.

NOTE:

Watch the texture, don't let it get pasty thick, and be absolutely sure that your flour and butter (roux) is cooked before adding the other ingredients. A common mistake is made when the roux is not completely cooked and the ending sauce is a sauce that tastes like uncooked flour. Learn to test your cooking through your sense of smell. You can easily tell when the flour has cooked completely when you get a bready aroma.

OYSTERS BIENVILLE

Sometimes called "Father of Louisiana," Jean Baptiste Le Moyne, Sieur de Bienville, was born in Montreal, Canada, in 1680. He entered the French navy while still a boy. He and his brother, Pierre Le Moyne, Sieur d'Iberville, went to France where Pierre was chosen to command the expedition for Louis XIV to found a colony in Louisiana. Jean Baptiste was appointed to accompany him and was eventually responsible for founding the settlement of New Orleans. He became an early governor of Louisiana.

This succulent dish named in his honor was originally created at Antoine's by Roy Alciatore and long-time chef, Auguste Michel. Michel said that one afternoon he and Mr. Roy were concocting some new dishes for an upcoming gourmet dinner at Antoine's. They put this one together and served it to the delight of their guests, one of whom was Arnaud Cazanave, the "Count," proprietor of Arnaud's Restaurant. The count took the dish back to his restaurant and it became known as Arnaud's dish, just as Oysters Rockefeller had already become Antoine's dish.

In no two restaurants will you find this dish prepared exactly the same way, but I do feel that the following recipe is the best.

3 dozen oysters in their liquor
Water

Poach the oysters in their own liquor for a minute, just until their edges begin to curl. Strain the oysters out of the liquid and set aside. Add enough water to the poaching liquor to bring it to 2 cups. Set aside.

Make the sauce.

Melt the butter in a saucepan and sauté the bell pepper, green onions, garlic and pimento until they are limp. Add the flour and cook together for two minutes. Blend in the white wine and the oyster liquor. Season with salt and pepper. Simmer for a few minutes until the sauce thickens. Fold in the cheese and bread crumbs and set aside to cool.

Assemble the dish.

Arrange the oysters in individual ovenproof dishes (6 per portion) and cover woth the Bienville sauce.

Bake in a preheated 375-degree oven for 15 minutes or until the sauce begins to brown on top. Serves 6.

VARIATIONS:

To begin with, you might want to hold out the cheeses and bread crumbs for a topping instead of incorporating it into the sauce. It is also popular to add chopped boiled shrimp and/or mushrooms.

NOTE:

This dish should be prepared "on the half-shell," but that is not the easiest thing to do at home. I prefer to prepare it in either individual soufflée-type cups or in a large casserole, spooned onto plates to serve.

If you do want to prepare these on the half-shell, you will need 6 pie pans filled with rock salt, and 36 half shells. Arrange 6 shells in a circle on each pan of salt, top with an oyster and cover with the sauce. Voila! The original and the most familiar restaurant presentation.

FOR THE SAUCE:

1 stick butter
1 bell pepper, seeded and minced
1 bunch green onions, chopped
2 toes garlic, minced
1 small jar pimento, minced
4 tablespoons flour
½ cup white wine, not too dry
1 teaspoon salt or to taste
½ teaspoon ground white pepper, or to taste
½ cup grated Swiss cheese
½ cup bread crumbs

SHRIMP MARINIERE

In the "fashion of sailors" would be how you might explain Mariniere. Again simplicity of the dish calls for good fresh shrimp. The original concept is French, as in Moules Mariniere. This is a more localized version.

2½ pounds medium shrimp
1¼ cups water
3 tablespoons butter
3 tablespoons flour
½ bunch chopped green
    onions
¼ cup white wine, not too
    dry
1 teaspoon salt
½ teaspoon ground white
    pepper
¼ teaspoon cayenne
2 egg yolks, beaten

Peel and devein the shrimp. Put the shells in a saucepan with 1½ cups water and boil for 5 minutes. Strain the water and set aside, discarding the shells.

Melt the butter and add the flour. Cook together for 2 minutes and add the chopped green onions. Continue cooking until the onions are limp, then add the white wine and the shrimp water. Bring to a boil. Season with the salt, pepper and cayenne. Add the raw shrimp and simmer just long enough that they are cooked through, about 3 minutes. Blend in the beaten yolks and heat without simmering until the sauce is thickened.

Spoon into small dishes and serve with French bread or toast for sopping up the sauce. Serves 6.

VARIATIONS:

Crayfish is the best substitute for the shrimp, but crabmeat and oysters also make excellent dishes.

Often the shrimp are pre-boiled before they are added to the sauce.

NOTE:

Remember—don't overcook the shrimp. They should have an almost crisp bite to them, never that mushy texture that we all too often find with frozen or overcooked shrimp.

OYSTERS BONNE FEMME

This is a dish that is often called "Oysters Pan Roast." Since there are any number of recipes for pan roast and since "Bonne Femme" is the classic Creole name for the dish, I use it here. *Bonne femme* means "good woman," befitting any woman who prepares this dish.

3 dozen shelled oysters in
    their liquor
3 tablespoons butter
3 tablespoons flour
1 bunch green onions,
    chopped
1 tablespoons minced
    parsley
½ cup white wine, not too
    dry
Salt and pepper to taste
1 pound crabmeat
¼ cup grated Swiss cheese
¼ cup grated Parmesan
    cheese
½ cup bread crumbs

Poach the oysters in their own liquor just long enough for their edges to begin to curl. Remove the pan from the heat and set aside.

In another saucepan, melt the butter and stir in the flour. Cook together for 2 minutes and add the green onions, parsley and white wine. Salt and pepper to taste.

Add the grated Swiss and Parmesan cheeses and the bread crumbs. Add the cooking liquor from the oysters and blend all together. When the mixture is hot add the crabmeat and oysters.

Heat for 2 minutes more, or until hot.

Spoon into small bowls or dishes and serve. Serves 6.

VARIATIONS:

The cheeses and bread crumbs can be held out of the mixture and sprinkled on top and baked to form a crust. It may be more desirable to have this separate texture in the dish.

This same preparation could be used with crayfish or shrimp or even as a sauce over poached fish.

NOTE:

The simplicity of the dish requires, as always, the use of good products. Use good crabmeat if it is available.

CHEESE STRAWS

The Creole ladies were often entertaining at home and had their own individual specialties that they served to their guests. Cheese straws is one of those little homemade savories that you could expect to find served with one's Sazerac Cocktail or Mint Julip. The color gives a plate of these delicacies the look of straw. They are a welcomed gift to bring to a friend's home when invited to cocktails.

In a bowl, cream the butter with the salt and cayenne. Blend in the cheddar and Parmesan. Add the flour and baking powder and work it all together well.

Roll the dough out on a floured surface to a thickness of ⅛ inch. Cut into 1- by 2-inch strips and place on an ungreased baking sheet. Bake in a preheated 325-degree oven for 20 minutes or until they crisp.

Cool and serve with cocktails. Makes about 4 dozen pieces.

1 stick butter
1 teaspoon salt
1 teaspoon cayenne
2 cups grated sharp
     cheddar cheese
¼ cup Parmesan cheese
1½ cups flour
1 teaspoon baking powder

VARIATIONS:

You might want to vary the amount of pepper to suit your own palate but Cheese Straws are traditionally spicy.

NOTE:

They should be kept in an airtight container to keep them fresh.

Soups, Bisques,
and Gumbo

CRAB AND CORN BISQUE

This is a delightful, soft luscious soup, easy to prepare and loved by all. It is actually an old Cajun recipe that has newly found its way to the city restaurants. The first time I had the soup was at Commander's Palace restaurant during the tenure of Paul Prudhomme. Since that time I have had it often and it always seems to come out quite palatable.

Cut the kernels from the ears of corn and set aside. Discard the cobs. Melt the butter in a heavy saucepan and blend in the flour. Cook together for 3 minutes. Add the minced green onions. Cook while stirring until the green onions soften, about 2 minutes. Whisk in the hot stock. Bring to a boil. Add the half and half and the corn. Season with salt and ground white pepper.

Bring to a boil and turn down to a simmer for about 20 minutes or until the liquid is reduced to about 1½ quarts.

Carefully fold in the crabmeat, adjust seasoning to taste, heat for just a minute more and serve. Serves 6 to 8.

6 ears fresh corn
½ cup butter
½ cup flour
½ bunch green onions, chopped
1 quart chicken stock
1 quart half and half
2 tablespoons salt
½ teaspoon ground white pepper
1 pound crabmeat

VARIATIONS:

Shrimp and even oysters make delicious variations to the crab. Crayfish also makes a dynamite bisque in this preparation.

NOTE:

It is important that you use fresh corn if you want the best soup.

CRAYFISH BISQUE

In my mind this is simply the classic Louisiana bisque. When properly prepared there is no dish that delivers the essence of Cajun cookery as this bisque does.

3 quarts water
2 pounds whole live
    crayfish
2 sticks butter
1 cup flour
1 large onion, chopped
1 bunch green onions,
    chopped
2 stalks celery, chopped
2 carrots, chopped
2 cloves garlic, minced
2 large tomatoes, skinned,
    seeded, and chopped
2 tablespoons minced
    parsley
¼ teaspoon thyme
2 bay leaves
2 tablespoons salt
1 teaspoon black pepper
½ teaspoon cayenne

Bring 3 quarts water to a boil. Add the live crayfish and bring back to a simmer. Remove the crayfish and set aside. Save the water and keep it hot.

Melt the butter in a large heavy saucepan. Blend in the flour and cook on a moderate heat, stirring constantly, until the "roux" has acquired a lovely brown color. Be careful that it is not burned or you will have to start over.

Add the chopped onions, green onions, celery, carrots, and garlic. Cook all together until the vegetables become limp.

Add the whole blanched crayfish to the pot and mash them completely using a blunt ended utensil like a rolling pin or a wooden mallet. It is very important that you do a good job here or you will not get the full richness and flavor of the crayfish into the bisque.

Add the chopped tomatoes, minced parsley, thyme, bay leaves and the reserved water. Add the salt, black pepper and cayenne. Bring to a boil. Cook at a low boil for 1 hour, stirring occasionally to prevent any sticking or burning.

Pass the soup through a strainer, forcing as much of the passable vegetable pulp and crayfish meat through as is possible. Discard the remaining mash. Bring the strained bisque back to a simmer and reduce to 1½ quarts or until the bisque reaches a rich, thick consistency. Remember that this is a bisque and not a soup and must be thick to be correct.

Adjust seasoning if necessary. Ladle into soupbowls and serve. Serves 6.

VARIATIONS:

This same recipe can be made with shrimp, crabs, or even lobsters since crayfish are seasonal.

Many people, instead of using the entire meat and shell in the bisque will remove the meat and use it as garnish in the soup or use the meat to make a stuffing for the crayfish heads, a few of which are put into each bowl as a sort of dumpling in the shell. In this case you can make a stuffing as the Oyster Stuffing for duck with the following changes: Quarter the recipe, as you will need a much smaller amount, and substitute crayfish for oysters. Roll the stuffed heads in bread crumbs and drop them in the soupbowls when serving.

NOTE:

This is a recipe whose preparation will vary drastically from one cook to another. Don't be surprised if you find opposing views to mine.

The texture should be quite hearty and thick, but if you find it too thick simply thin it with some water or chicken bouillon.

GUMBO

No two cooks will agree on the same ingredients for the true and proper gumbo. Don't bother, I have tried for years to come up with what I consider the "original" gumbo, yet the first person I try it out on argues with me about it.

I have resigned myself to living my life without another single person believing that I am correct. Unless it is someone who has never tasted any gumbo but mine.

There are two basic types of gumbo: okra gumbo and filé gumbo. Some might argue that there is a third—Gumbo Z'Herbes. This is actually more of a stew made from greens. Gumbo Z'Herbes was devised for use during Lent or fasting periods.

In Okra Gumbo, it is the okra that is used as both a flavoring and thickening agent. (The African word for okra is *gombo*.)

The preparation of gumbo always begins with a roux. Next, you add the vegetables including the okra. From there you can let your imagination fly and add almost any ingredient you want. But, no matter what you add, you still have an okra gumbo. You might make it a seafood gumbo, or a chicken and andouille gumbo, or whatever you want—it is still an okra gumbo.

Gumbo filé is ground sassafras leaves. The addition of the filé accomplishes several things at once. First, it has a musty, earthy flavor. Second, it a thickening agent—it acts quickly, but tends to become viscous when left to heat for too long a period. Third it darkens and enriches the color of the gumbo, bringing it to that deep brown-green typical of the dish. Many restaurants don't use it in the cooking, but, rather put a bottle of it on the table with the other condiments to be added by the diner.

Purists would say that you have one or the other, okra or filé, but not both ingredients in the same pot. I used to be a purist, but I gave up that position when I stopped attempting to convince people that I knew what the "true" gumbo was. Now, I use them both together as often as I have them both to use. After all, the end goal is to produce the best tasting dish you can. Using both is the way I attempt to accomplish this feat for myself and my guests.

Anyone wanting to develop a repertoire of Louisiana dishes should learn a gumbo first. It is the single most important dish in all of Louisiana cookery.

2 pounds whole shrimp

10 cups water

2 teaspoons salt

1 stick butter (¼ pound)

½ cup flour

1 large white onion, chopped

1 bunch green onions, chopped

½ cup chopped celery

1½ cups chopped okra (or 1 ten ounce package frozen)

1 tablespoon minced parsley

1 pound andouille sausage (or any spicy smoked sausage available)

3 crabs, top shells and lungs removed

1 teaspoon black pepper

½ teaspoon cayenne pepper

Salt to taste

1 rounded tablespoon filé powder

4 cups hot cooked rice

Peel and head the shrimp, put the meat aside. Put the water, salt, and shrimp peels and heads into a soup pot and bring to a boil. Continue boiling for approximately 30 minutes, or until the water has been reduced to about 3 cups. Strain out the shells and reserve the liquid. Set aside.

Add the butter to a large soup pot and melt. Add the flour and cook and stir constantly until the mixture, the "roux," becomes a nutty brown color. Add the chopped white onion, green onions, celery, and okra. Continue cooking until they brown.

Add the parsley and sliced sausage and cook for about 5 minutes. Blend the reserved shrimp liquor into the ingredients. Bring to a boil, reduce to a simmer, and continue cooking for approximately 30 minutes. Add the shrimp and cook for 2 minutes more. Blend in the filé powder. Put ½ cup hot, cooked rice in large soup bowls and ladle the gumbo into the bowls. Serves 6 to 8.

VARIATIONS:

The variations to gumbo are simply endless. Some of the more popular combinations are the following: shrimp, crab and oyster gumbo, duck and sausage gumbo, chicken and oyster gumbo, turkey gumbo. Use whatever you want.

NOTE:

Thickness of the soup can be lessened by adding more water.

OYSTER SOUP

Probably the simplest of all the soups and bisques is this Oyster Soup. It is favored by many as a good homemade dish. I remember it as a favorite dish in our home when I was a child. I used to watch my mother make it at the stove in what seemed a very short time for such a delicious soup.

Later I remember it at festive brunches and particularly at Brennan's Restaurant.

Melt the butter in a large saucepan and sauté the celery and green onions until they are limp, about 3 minutes. Blend in the flour and cook for 2 minutes more. Add the garlic, parsley, and bay leaves. Blend in the oyster water and milk mixture. Bring to a boil and reduce to a simmer. Season with the salt and pepper. Simmer for 15 minutes. Add the oysters and simmer for only about 5 minutes more and serve. Serves 6 to 8.

VARIATIONS:

The milk may make the soup a little too rich for some tastes. Fish or chicken stock can be used for subtle and delightful variation.

NOTE:

The thickness of this soup can be changed if desired by the addition of extra liquid, either milk or of any of the possible substitutions listed above.

1 stick butter
1 rib celery, minced
1 bunch green onions, chopped
6 tablespoons flour
1 large clove garlic, minced
1 tablespoon minced parsley
2 bay leaves
1½ quarts liquid (the liquor from the oysters and enough milk to bring it to 1½ quarts)
2 teaspoons salt
1 teaspoon ground white pepper
2 dozen raw oysters

OYSTER AND ARTICHOKE SOUP

Though oysters and artichokes are a traditional combination in Louisiana cookery, it was Warren LeRuth at LeRuth's Restaurant, who made this soup first available to the present generation of epicures.

4 whole fresh artichokes
2 quarts water
1 tablespoon salt

4 tablespoons butter
4 tablespoons flour
1 large onion, chopped
½ bunch green onions, chopped
½ teaspoon thyme
1 stalk celery, minced
2 bay leaves
Salt and pepper to taste
1 quart fresh oysters in their water

Put the artichokes, salt, and water into a saucepan and bring to a boil. Continue boiling until the stems of the artichokes are tender, about 30 to 45 minutes.

In another pot heat the butter and combine it with the flour. Cook, stirring constantly for about 3 minutes. Add the white and green onions and let them cook just enough to soften. Pour the water in which the artichokes have been boiled into the pot of ingredients. Add the thyme, minced celery, and bay leaves. Bring to a boil and turn down to a simmer.

Clean the artichokes and slice the hearts and stems into thin strips. Scrape the meat from the leaves. Add the artichoke strips and the meat from the leaves to the pot. Strain the liquid from the oysters and add the liquid to the pot. Season with salt and pepper and simmer for 20 minutes.

Add the oysters only a few minutes before you are ready
to serve the soup. When you add the oysters, continue to
cook only long enough for the edges of the oysters to begin
to curl. If you cook the oysters too long they will become
tough.

Ladle into soupbowls and serve. Serves 6 to 8.

VARIATIONS:

Varying combinations of seafoods and vegetables is essential to our repertoire. Try eggplants or Jerusalem artichokes, or alternate shrimp or crayfish for the oysters.

NOTE:

It is highly important to use the fresh artichokes in this
soup. Canned hearts will produce only a pale copy of what
this soup should taste like.

But then again, if it is simplicity that you desire in this
preparation, canned artichoke hearts are better than none
at all.

RED BEAN SOUP

Red bean soup had come to be a dish that reminds me of chilly afternoons in the fall, romance by candlelight, full warm feelings inside, and lovely, sweet memories of a far less complicated time of my life.

Although it is sometimes made from the leftovers of Monday's red beans and rice, I prefer to make it from scratch in a batch big enough to keep some in the freezer. And it is a wonderful rich warm soup for especially cold days in the winter.

1 pound red beans
4 quarts water
2 cups chopped onions
½ cup chopped bell pepper
½ cup chopped celery
2 tablespoons minced garlic
3 bay leaves
½ teaspoon thyme
2 tablespoons minced
    parsley
½ teaspoon chili powder
1 teaspoon black pepper
½ teaspoon cayenne pepper
1 tablespoon salt
3 tablespoons vinegar
3 smoked ham hocks
    (6 to 8 ounces each,
    1 pound ham)
Sherry
2 lemons sliced into thin
    rounds

Put all the ingredients together with the water in a large soup pot and bring to a boil. Turn down to a simmer, cover the pot, and continue cooking for three hours, stirring occasionally to be sure that nothing sticks to the bottom and scorches. If the soup becomes too thick, add more water. After three hours take the soup off the fire. Remove the ham hocks and set aside. Pass the soup through a strainer, being careful to force all of the pulp through, and put it back on the fire. Remove the meat from the hocks and add it to the soup. Adjust seasoning if necessary. Bring back to simmer.

To serve, ladle the soup into bowls and add a dash of sherry. Float a round of sliced lemon on top and you are ready.

This recipe could serve six to eight as a main course, if accompanied with a salad and french bread, or twelve as a beginning course. I have determined this amount because it employs the whole pound of red beans, which is the way they are generally packed. Somehow, partial packs of red beans seem to remain forever in my kitchen cabinet, and eventually everywhere but in the bag they came in. If you don't use all the soup in one serving, freeze it for another

occasion when you don't have three hours to slave over a
hot stove. This is when the cook will enjoy it the most.

VARIATIONS:

The variations are as many different sorts of dried beans
and peas as you can find. White northerns and black beans
are the most often used substitutes.

The hocks can be exchanged for another seasoning meat
like ham or salt pork, or pickled pork, or hot sausage.

NOTE:

The sherry and lemon are not absolutely necessary but
they do carry this soup to a far more sophisticated level of
taste and cookery. Use them if you have them.

Thickness can be adjusted by using more or less water.

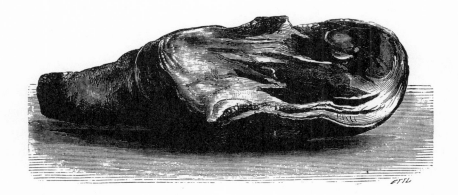

TURTLE SOUP

Turtle soup is a true standard of the New Orleans restaurant menu and one enjoyed by everyone. The actual species of turtle used varies from green sea turtle (now endangered), to snapping turtles and terrapins. There was a time when the soft shell turtle was also used and you actually ate the shell.

When the standard commercial meat of the green sea turtle became unavailable a few years back for conservation reasons, some of us switched to alligator meat, which had recently become legal game again. There are many who prefer not to deal with any of these creatures and produce a fine "mock" turtle soup using heavy veal or beef.

In a large saucepan or soup pot, melt the butter and blend in the flour. Cook together, stirring occassionally, until the mixture, the roux, obtains a light brown color.

Add the chopped onions and turtle meat. Cook, stirring often to prevent sticking or burning, until the onions and turtle meat are browned. Add the minced celery, and chopped tomato pulp and simmer together for fifteen minutes. Cut the lemon in half, squeeze and reserve the juice, discard the seeds, and mince the lemon rind. Add the lemon juice and minced rind along with all remaining ingredients, except the sherry, to the pot. Simmer slowly for 1½ hours. Rectify seasoning with salt and black pepper. To serve, splash about a tablespoon of sherry in the bottom of each soup bowl and ladle in the soup. Serves 6 to 8, depending on the size of the soup bowls.

VARIATIONS:

This same soup can be made with any number of variations; instead of turtle meat you could use alligator meat or heavy veal, and use 2 pounds of meat instead of 1 if you want a heartier soup.

Many people like to add chopped hard-boiled eggs to this soup. Traditionally, the eggs of the turtle were used in the soup along with the meat. If you want to use eggs, add 3 chopped hard-boiled eggs at the end of the cooking.

NOTE:

If you use a salty stock to begin with, be very careful when adding any addtional salt.

1 stick butter
½ cup flour
2 onions, chopped
2 pounds turtle meat, cut into ½-inch cubes
2 stalks celery, minced
2 tomatoes, skinned, seeded, and finely chopped
1 lemon
½ teaspoon thyme
1 tablespoon minced parsley
3 cloves garlic, minced
2 bay leaves
4 whole cloves
1 lemon
1 teaspoon black pepper
½ teaspoon cayenne
1½ quarts beef stock
Salt and black pepper to taste, at end of cooking
⅓ cup sherry

Fish and Seafood

BARBEQUED SHRIMP

Manale's restaurant in New Orleans carries the distinction of having created the original version of barbequed shrimp, now a standard on New Orleans restaurant menus. Every cook and chef has his own recipe for this dish and every dish varies. I offer the following as what I believe that original version to be. This preparation is in fact not barbequed at all but was so named by its creator.

In a wide saucepan or skillet melt the butter and add the pepper and salt. Heat for 2 minutes to give the pepper a moment to develop. Add the shrimp and cook only long enough for the shrimp to be cooked through yet still have a nice bite to the texture of the meat, 6 to 8 minutes. Spoon into bowls and serve with french bread for sopping up the sauce. Serves 6.

1 pound butter
4 tablespoons freshly
    ground black pepper
4 tablespoons salt
4½ pounds large shrimp,
    head and shell on
    (approximately 12
    ounces per portion)
French bread

VARIATIONS:

Any shellfish will do well in this preparation.
   A touch of cayenne would do nicely and a squeeze of lemon.

NOTE:

Don't overcook the shrimp! You don't want them mushy; good texture is important in this dish.
   Headless shrimp will not make as good a dish because you will not get the fat and juices from the head that make the simple butter sauce so good.

BLACKENED REDFISH

Not since my great-grandfather, Jules Alciatore, invented Oysters Rockefeller at Antoine's Restaurant in 1899, has a local culinary creation received such widespread acclaim as has Blackened Redfish. A bookdealer friend of mine said to me of Paul Prudhomme, its creator, "Paul's star is crossing the sky. And flying right alongside is his Blackened Redfish."

I understand the dish and I like it for several reasons. First, I am always the one in the kitchen picking out the crispy pieces from the bottom of the pot or pan, whether it be roast, or gratinée vegetables, or something overcooked in the fry. Even with toast—if there are several pieces I will choose the darkest. There was a gentleman that used to dine regularly with us at Antoine's. He ordered his french bread toasted to the degree of charred blackness. His theory was that it helped filter out the alcohol in the several martinis he had before dinner, and also, he just plain liked it that way. With the waiters he got the nickname of "the burnt bread man." The only problem with serving him blackened bread was that unknowing diners in the vicinity of his table thought that the waiter was being completely careless and totally unprofessional. So, his waiter would be required to make the rounds of the neighboring tables explaining that this was the way that our friend wanted his bread.

That charred taste can be quite delicious. There is a method that we use to cook steak that we call "Indian Style." To prepare a steak Indian Style you put it on a fireproof plate and place the plate under the broiler or salamander (restaurant term for broiler). The plate is then lifted up so that the meat actually touches the flame from the gas jets and is charred black. This is done on both sides, then the steak is served with a little melted butter. The charred taste is quite agreeable, and the process sears the meat, encasing the steak in its own outer crust, and sealing in all the juices that might be cooked out in a more lengthy cooking. And char-broiled hamburgers are certainly not new to the American public.

The same thing happens with Blackened Redfish. The flesh of the fish is sealed in the charring in the white hot iron skillet, and the juices retained. Paul, however, has added the dimension of spices to enhance and flavor the fish, thus developing the depth of flavor to new heights.

Years before Blackened Redfish appeared on the scene, Paul was working with the Brennans at Commander's Palace Restaurant. One of the dishes that appeared on the menu during his tenure there was Filet Debris. Now, Filet Debris was a grilled filet of beef served with a salty, rich, pan drippings sauce that was just that—pan drippings. In the drippings were the little crispy pieces of charred meat that make their way into the gravy. Whenever I prepare a roast, it is these pieces that I look for as the tastiest part of the dish, and cook's privilege to enjoy. Paul recognized his own sense of taste as valid, and followed through with it to great success.

There is one more aspect of the taste of this dish that I feel has contributed to its great success. Many people from areas of the country who are not as used to a regular diet of seafood as we are in Louisiana, might tend to like this particular preparation because the resulting taste is not "fishy." The char and the spices give it a taste that might even be reminiscent of a poultry or meat dish, thus appealing to a wider group of individual tastes. Whatever the combination is, it works!

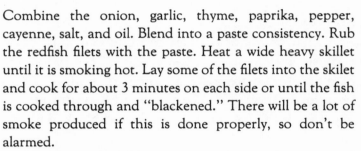

1 small onion, finely
    minced
2 cloves garlic, finely
    minced
1 teaspoon thyme
1 teaspoon paprika
1 teaspoon black pepper
1 teaspoon cayenne
1 tablespoon salt
¼ cup peanut oil
6 six to eight ounce redfish
    filets
2 sticks butter

Combine the onion, garlic, thyme, paprika, pepper, cayenne, salt, and oil. Blend into a paste consistency. Rub the redfish filets with the paste. Heat a wide heavy skillet until it is smoking hot. Lay some of the filets into the skilet and cook for about 3 minutes on each side or until the fish is cooked through and "blackened." There will be a lot of smoke produced if this is done properly, so don't be alarmed.

Place the cooked fish on a warm plate in the oven until you have cooked all the filets. Put the 2 sticks butter into the same skillet and melt. You want the blackened herbs in the skillet in the butter so scrape them up with a wood spoon.

Put the fish on plates and spoon over the melted butter. Serves 6.

VARIATIONS:

Trout and pompano both make excellent substitutes for the redfish. Any strong textured fish that you may have available will work well.

NOTE:

This recipe can be difficult to do at home as the skillet needs on a hot fire to work perfectly. But don't fear. This makes an excellent dish on any fire, even if you don't get the full blackening effect.

Be sure that your vent is turned on for this dish.

CORNMEAL FRIED OYSTERS

This is the most traditional method of frying oysters. Here we use cayenne enough to get a bite of pepperiness.

Blend the cornmeal, salt, black pepper, and cayenne together. Heat the oil in a frying skillet to a moderate-hot temperature, 375 degrees. Roll the oysters in the cornmeal and fry in the oil until golden brown. Drain on paper and serve with lemon wedges. Serves 6.

2 cups cornmeal
1 tablespoon salt
1 teaspoon black pepper
½ teaspoon cayenne
Oil, enough to give you
    a depth of 1 inch
    in the pan
4 dozen raw oysters
3 lemons, cut into wedges

VARIATIONS:

Use regular flour or cornflour in place of the cornmeal. There are so many preferences it will be up to your own taste to find your favorite. All are good.

NOTE:

The Creoles used to use french bread crumbs or cracker crumbs for their breading, both of which make delicious fried oysters that you may want to try at home.

OYSTERS EN BROCHETTE

The "brochette," or skewer, used in the cooking of the oysters gives this dish its name. Any meat, seafood, or vegetable prepared in this fashion could be called "en brochette." The method consists of placing several pieces of the meat on a skewer to hold them together while cooking. Oysters and bacon on a skewer, battered and fried, make a wonderful combination.

21 strips of bacon
    (1 pound)
1 cup milk
1 egg
1½ cups flour
2 teaspoons salt
1 teaspoon ground black
    pepper
½ teaspoon cayenne pepper
36 oysters
3 lemons cut into wedges

Cut the strips of bacon crosswise into three pieces each and fry. Drain on paper. Take two mixing bowls. Mix the milk and eggs together in one and the flour, salt, pepper, and cayenne together in the other. Load the skewers, alternating bacon and 6 oysters ending with a extra bacon (7 pieces).

Heat the oil in a frying pan until it is hot but not smoking. Dip the brochettes in the milk and egg wash and then dredge them in the seasoned flour mix. Fry golden on both sides. Drain on paper and serve with lemon wedges for squeezing. Serves 6

VARIATIONS:

Shrimp is the best substitute for oysters in this dish.

This recipe can also be made without the batter by simply grilling the oyster-bacon combination on the skewer and serving with lemon and melted butter.

A Hollandaise sauce with the basic recipe would also be quite tasty.

NOTE:

The oysters must be fresh and the bacon should be fairly lean in order to stay on the skewer.

Be sure that the batter is completely cooked and not too heavy in the areas between the oysters.

POMPANO EN PAPILLOTE OR POMPANO IN A PAPER BAG

Pompano in a Paper Bag, although the dish is another one of Antoine's many creations, is not, as a means of cooking, a New Orleans invention.

The method of wrapping foods in parchment or in some sort of leaf vegetable is a process almost as old as cooking itself and can be found in the cooking of many countries. I have had many dishes cooked "en papillote," from salmon, to chicken to veal chops. It is a very good method of cooking because it holds in all the flavors that generally escape during the cooking process. It is also an easy way to cook, particularly for amateurs, because the paper browns but not the food, so there is less chance of burning the food inside. And it makes a rather nice presentation to bring the cooked papillotes to the table and open them in front of the guests to let the wonderful aromas escape right before their very noses.

This dish was first prepared at Antoine's for a visiting French balloonist. The intention was to have the vapor-filled papillote have the appearance of a balloon.

Poach the fish:

Put the water into a wide shallow saucepan with the sliced onion, sliced lemon, the chopped celery, the bay leaves, 6 whole black peppercorns, 2 teaspoons salt, ½ cup white wine and 1 quart water, or enough to cover the filets.

Bring to a boil and add the pompano filets. Poach gently until the filets are cooked, about 5 minutes. Remove the pompano filets to a warm platter and reduce the liquid to 2 cups. Strain.

Make the sauce:

In another saucepan, heat the butter and add the flour. Cook together, for three minutes and add the chopped green onions. Continue cooking until the onions become limp, five minutes, and then blend in 1 cup white wine and the 2 cups reduced poaching liquid.

Bring to a boil, turn down to a simmer and simmer for ten minutes or until the sauce reaches a fairly thick consistency. Add the raw peeled shrimp and simmer for one minute more, or only long enough for the shrimp to turn pink. Remove from the fire and fold in the crabmeat. Let cool.

1 onion, sliced
1 lemon, sliced
1 rib celery, chopped
2 bay leaves
6 whole black peppercorns
2 teaspoon salt
½ cup white wine
1 quart water
6 six-ounce pieces of pompano fillet

FOR THE SAUCE:
6 tablespoons butter
6 tablespoons flour
1 bunch chopped green onions
1 cup white wine, not too dry
2 cups reduced and reserved poaching liquor
1 pound small raw shrimp, peeled
1 pound lump crabmeat
Cooking parchment, waxed paper, or tin foil
Butter

Assemble the dish:

Cut 6 heart shapes from the parchment paper, 10 inches high and 14 inches wide. Lay them out flat and butter them. When the sauce is cool and not runny, spoon it onto one side of each heart. Top each with a pompano filet.

Fold the the other side of the heart over and fold the edges together all the way around the open side. Place the papillotes on a buttered baking pan and into a preheated 400-degree oven for 15 to 20 minutes or until the paper browns. Remove to serving dishes.

To serve, bring to the table and using two forks, tear and fold open the papillote across the length of the top. Serves 6.

VARIATIONS:

You can use aluminum foil instead of the parchment. It works as well or better than the parchment. And since the foil is so easy to fold you don't even have to cut it into a heart shape; use 10 $\times$ 14-inch rectangles.

White freezer paper can also be used, but be sure that if it's the waxed kind you keep the waxed side on the outside. You don't want your sauce to taste like candles. After baking be careful in transferring the papillotes to serving plates. Lift them carefully with a spatula. Don't tear them!

Because the texture of the fish does not have to survive any hard cooking like grilling or frying you can use any fish in this preparation. Just be sure the filet is poached all the way through before you put it into the parchment.

You might want to add oysters instead of, or even with, the shrimp. Or you may add mushrooms, cooked as you would cook the shrimp.

If you want to bake the fish without poaching, put the raw filet into the paper with the sauce the same way but bake at 350 degrees for about 30 minutes.

Chicken, veal, lamb, pork, anything almost at all can be cooked "en Papillote."

NOTE:

Try this for yourself first until you become comfortable with the process. It's a great genre of cooking to have in your repertoire.

REDFISH COURTBOUILLON

Courtbouillon comes from French meaning "short boil" and refers to any aromatic liquid in which fish, meat, or vegetables are cooked. The broth is generally served as part of the dish as opposed to discarding it after cooking. Our Creole Courtbouillon is a bit heavier than the traditional French. In our dish, the liquid becomes more of a sauce and is served over the fish.

1 stick butter
4 tablespoons flour
1 large onion, chopped
1 bunch green onions, chopped
2 cloves garlic, minced
3 large tomatoes, chopped
½ cup red wine
2 cups water or fish stock
½ teaspoon thyme
½ teaspoon marjoram
3 bay leaves
¼ teaspoon powdered allspice
1 lemon, thinly sliced, seeds removed
2 tablespoons salt
1 teaspoon black pepper
½ teaspoon cayenne
6 redfish filets, 6 to 8 ounces each

Melt the butter in a wide, deep saucepan and add the flour. Cook together until the flour becomes light brown in color. This is the roux.

Add the onions, celery, green onions, and garlic and continue cooking until the onions are limp. This should only take 5 or 6 minutes.

Add the chopped tomatoes, the wine, water, all the seasoning spices and herbs, and the lemon slices. Simmer together for 20 minutes. Adjust seasonings.

Lay the red fish filets into the sauce and simmer until they are cooked through, about 20 minutes. Test the fish with a fork to be sure it is white and flaky all the way through. Adjust seasoning and serve. Serves 6.

VARIATIONS:

Many cooks prefer to use a whole fish, 4 to 5 pounds. In this case you would prepare the sauce as above and pour it over the fish and bake covered in a 325-degree oven for about 45 minutes. If you buy a whole fish and filet it yourself, you will have the bones, head and scraps with which to make a little stock. All you have to do is boil these in a quart of water until the water is reduced to 2 cups. Use this as your stock instead of just water.

Any large white fleshy fish can be substituted here—red snapper, haddock, swordfish.

Some cooks prefer to use filets of fish and season them with salt and pepper and dredge in flour, and fry in the butter at the beginning. The fry batter does give the dish an added dimension.

NOTE:

Do this one for a crowd and bring the whole fish (if you use one) to the table for a little fanfare while you serve.

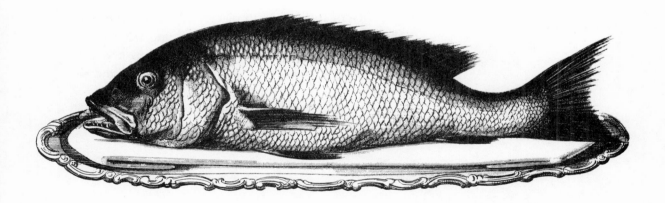

POMPANO PONTCHARTRAIN

This is named after our own Lake Pontchartrain, from which much of the seafood used in New Orleans is taken.

1 pound butter
2 pounds good lump
    crabmeat

½ cup oil, not olive
1 tablespoon salt
1 teaspoon ground white
    pepper
6 six to eight-ounce
    pompano filets
6 sprigs parsley
3 lemons, halved

Melt the butter in a heavy saucepan and add the crabmeat. Disturb the crabmeat as little as possible so as not to break up the lumps. Keep warm.

Blend the oil with the salt and pepper and rub it onto the pompano filets. Cook the filets on a hot grill or in a heavy iron skillet for 3 minutes on each side, or until done. Place the cooked filets on dinner plates and spoon the hot crabmeat and butter mixture over the top.

Garnish with parsley and lemon halves.

VARIATIONS:

Any fish filet can be used in place of the pompano here.

Shrimp can be used in place of the lump crabmeat.

Some people prefer to sauté some chopped green onions in the butter with a little white wine before adding the crabmeat.

This dish was originally prepared with a small soft-shell crab called a "buster" instead of the lump crabmeat.

SHRIMP CREOLE

Shrimp Creole is a dish that I have been eating at the family table at least once a week for my entire life. The sauce is the essence of Creole cookery, and more the product of the Spanish influence in our local culture than that of the French, though the dish is reminiscent of some French Provençal dishes.

In a large skillet or saucepan, melt the butter and sauté the onions and bell peppers until they become limp. Add the chopped tomatoes and all remaining ingredients except the shrimp, rice, and sprig parsley. Simmer together just long enough to eliminate excess liquid. Add the shrimp and continue cooking for a few minutes, or until the shrimp become fully but not over cooked.

Serve each portion over ½ cup rice and garnish with parsley sprigs. Serves 6 to 8.

VARIATIONS:

Chicken Creole, which I have included in this collection, is also popular. This recipe also works well with crayfish and lump crabmeat.

NOTE:

I personally do not at all like Creole sauces that have been cooked to death and resemble a worn out Italian tomato sauce. I believe that it is vital for the vegetables to still be distinguishable from one another in both taste and texture.

2 tablespoons butter
3 large onions, rough chopped
2 large bell peppers, seeded and rough chopped
6 large tomatoes, skinned and seeded, rough chopped
¼ teaspoon thyme leaves
3 bay leaves
1 teaspoon paprika
4 cloves garlic, minced
2 tablespoons minced parsley
2 teaspoons salt, or to taste
½ teaspoon black pepper
¼ teaspoon cayenne pepper, or to taste
3 pounds whole raw shrimp, peeled and headed
3 cups hot cooked rice
Parsley sprigs for garnish

SHRIMP ETOUFFÉE

The word *étouffer* means to braise or to smother. In Louisiana cookery it definitely means to smother. As popular a dish done with crayfish as shrimp, "etouffee" represents an entire genre of cooking.

Shrimp or crayfish etouffee is a country dish and should be spicy.

1½ cups rice
3 cups water
1 tablespoon butter
1 teaspoon salt

Cook the rice:

Put 3 cups water in a saucepan with 1 tablespoon butter and 1 teaspoon salt and bring to a boil. Add 1½ cups rice. Bring the water to a simmer, cover and cook at a low simmer for about 20 minutes or until all the water is absorbed. Hold aside and keep warm.

Cook the shrimp:

Peel and devein the shrimp. Set aside, discard the veins, and mash the heads and shells in the bottom of a heavy saucepan using a blunt utensil such as a rolling pin or wooden mallet. Add approximately 1 quart of water to the pot and bring to a boil. Let boil for 20 minutes. Strain and discard the shells and reduce the liquid to 3 cups. This becomes a shrimp stock.

Make the sauce:

Heat the butter in a heavy skillet and blend in the flour. Cook together, stirring constantly until the roux acquires a golden color. Add the onion, celery, bell pepper and green onions. Cook together until all has browned. Add the 3 cups shrimp stock. Add the thyme, paprika, cayenne, bay leaves, garlic, and tomato paste. Add the salt, black pepper, and cayenne. Bring to a boil, turn down to a simmer, and continue cooking until it has acquired a thick saucy texture.

Add the raw shrimp and cook just long enough for them to be barely cooked all the way through. Adjust seasoning. Serve each portion over hot cooked rice. Serves 6.

VARIATIONS:

I have already discussed crayfish which is the best. I have made fish etouffee that came out to be quite enjoyable. When crayfish are out of season and good shrimp are hard to come by, try the same preparation with fish filet, cut into 1-inch cubes and deep fried in a batter.

NOTE:

Remember: Don't overcook. The shrimp, crayfish or fish should retain a good texture.

3 pounds fresh whole small shrimp
1½ quarts water
1 stick butter
½ cup flour
1 large onion, chopped
2 ribs celery, minced
1 small bell pepper, seeded and chopped
1 bunch green onions, chopped
½ teaspoon thyme
½ teaspoon paprika
3 bay leaves
¼ teaspoon cayenne
2 toes garlic, minced
1 tablespoon tomato paste
2 tablespoon salt
½ teaspoon black pepper

SPICY CORNMEAL FRIED CATFISH

This dish is one that comes from Manchac, Louisiana, which is about 20 minutes from New Orleans. It is an area where much of the seafood, catfish, and turtle come from to supply New Orleans. There are restaurants in this still small town that specialize in catfish prepared in this manner.

Years ago, before catfish was a popular fish to serve, it was sold in these restaurants as "thinfish," which was actually thinly sliced filet of catfish. The cornmeal helped greatly in diminishing the sometimes "muddy" taste of the large lake catfish.

Even now with the advent of farmed catfish and the growing acceptability of those light and fresh-tasting fish this preparation still stands out as a winner.

If you want it to be authentic you must make it spicy as I have it here.

1 cup milk
1 egg
1½ cups finely ground
     cornmeal
2 teaspoons salt
1 teaspoon ground black
     pepper
½ teaspoon cayenne
Vegetable oil, enough to
     get a ½ inch depth in
     the frying pan, about
     2 cups
3 lemons, cut into 4 wedges
     each
Catfish filets

Take 2 mixing bowls. Blend the milk and eggs in one and the cornmeal, salt, black pepper, and cayenne in the other. Pour enough oil to get a depth of ½ inch in a large frying pan and heat the oil until it's hot but not smoking.

Dip the catfish filets in the milk and egg wash and then dredge them in the seasoned cornmeal. Fry on both sides until they are golden.

Remove and drain on paper and serve with lots of lemons for squeezing. Serves 6.

VARIATIONS:

Shrimp, crayfish or any other kind of fish works well. This recipe is meant to be very peppery. The same without all the cayenne is good also.

A seafood cocktail sauce or tartar sauce will go well with this preparation.

NOTE:

Don't let the cornmeal cook too brown. It should end up nicely golden and crisp.

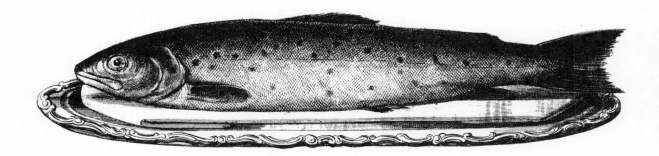

TROUT FLORENTINE

This is a very elegant dish which I would place in the category of Haute Creole. This is a dish that you might want to save for a very special evening with guests who enjoy rich food.

2 ten-ounce bags of fresh
   spinach
2 tablespoons butter
3 tablespoons butter
3 tablespoons flour
1 cup hot milk
2 teaspoons salt
1 teaspoon pepper

Make the creamed spinach:

Wash the spinach and discard the tough stem pieces. Chop the leaves. Melt 2 tablespoons butter in a large saucepan and add the spinach. Cover the pot and simmer for about 15 minutes or until the spinach becomes limp.

In a small saucepan melt 3 tablespoons butter and blend in the flour. Stir and cook for 2 minutes without coloring the flour. Whisk in 1 cup hot milk. Season with salt and pepper and simmer until thickened. Pour the cream sauce into the spinach and blend together and simmer for 2 minutes more or until all is well thickened. Adjust seasonings. Set aside and keep warm.

Make the hollandaise:

Put the egg yolks, lemon juice, salt, and cayenne in the top part of a double boiler. Cut the butter sticks in half and add 1 of the 6 pieces to the egg yolk mixture. Heat the water in the bottom of the double boiler without ever letting it come to a boil. Whisk the mixture until the butter is completely melted. Add the next piece. Continue this process until you have used all the butter pieces. Keep whisking over the heat until the sauce has thickened. Remove from heat and continue whisking until the sauce has cooled slightly. Keep warm.

Poach the trout filets:

Pour the water into a wide shallow saucepan. Add the onion, lemon, peppercorns, salt, bay leaves, and thyme. Bring to a simmer. Add the trout filets and simmer for 5 minutes or until they are completely cooked. Remove to a warm platter.

Assemble the dish:

Spoon the creamed spinach into 6 individual ovenproof dishes. Place a filet of poached trout on each bed of creamed spinach. Spoon the hollandaise over the filets. Sprinkle the grated cheeses and bread crumbs over the hollandaise. Bake in a preheated 400-degree oven until the cheese is melted and the top begins to brown. Serves 6.

FOR THE HOLLANDAISE:

6 egg yolks
3 tablespoons lemon juice
1 teaspoon salt
¼ teaspoon cayenne
3 sticks butter

1½ quarts water
1 sliced onion
1 sliced lemon
6 whole peppercorns
1 tablespoon salt
2 bay leaves
¼ teaspoon thyme
6 four to six-ounce pieces
    of trout filets
¼ cup grated Swiss cheese
¼ cup grated Parmesan
    cheese
½ cup bread crumbs

VARIATIONS:

The best variation of this dish is done with eggs replacing the trout. I have that recipe included in this collection.

NOTE:

This is a very rich dish and one that should be served as a complete meal. The spinach base and the hollandaise are going to leave your appetite with room for little else.

You could actually prepare and assemble this dish in advance and keep it covered in the refrigerator until you are ready for final preparations. In this case, bake the cold Trout Florentine in a 350-degree oven for about 30 minutes or until the trout is completely cooked and the top is browned.

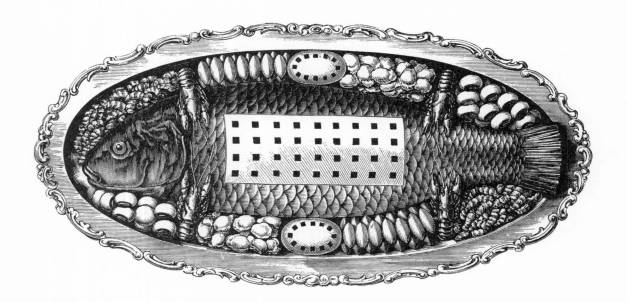

TROUT AMANDINE

One of the simplest and most popular dishes in this repertoire. This preparation seems to be well liked and can also be made with pecans instead of the almonds.

Sauté the sliced almonds in butter until they become golden brown. Set aside and keep warm.

Take two bowls and combine the eggs and milk in one and the salt pepper and flour in the other. Pour oil into a large frying pan to a depth of about ¼ inch. Heat the oil until it is hot but not smoking. Lay the trout filets into the oil and fry to a golden brown on one side and then the other. This will take about 10 minutes.

Drain the trout filets on paper. To serve, put a filet on each plate and spoon over the hot almonds and butter. Serves 6.

1½ cup sliced almonds
2 sticks butter
2 whole eggs
1 cup milk
2 teaspoons salt
1 teaspoon pepper
1 cup flour
6 trout filets, 6 ounces each
Oil for frying

VARIATIONS:

Pecans are the most common substitute for the almonds, but walnuts also make a delicious preparation.

Almost any available fish can be used here.

NOTE:

It is important that the nuts are browned to get that extra nutty taste that makes the dish so delicious. Don't overcook the nuts, however, as is possible, especially with the softer nuts like pecans.

TROUT MARGUERY

The original Marguery sauce was created by a Monsieur Mangin, who was the chef for thirty years of the famous Restaurant Marguery in Paris. That restaurant has been closed for many years, but the dish remains a part of culinary history. In its original form the Marguery sauce was prepared to serve with sole and garnished with mussels and shrimp. This Louisiana variation employs shrimp and mushrooms. It is somewhat of a specialty at Galatoire's Restaurant.

1½ to 2 quarts water,
    enough to cover filets
1 sliced onion
1 sliced lemon
12 whole peppercorns
1 tablespoon salt
2 bay leaves
¼ teaspoon thyme
6 six-ounce trout filets

FOR THE SAUCE:
1 stick butter
4 tablespoons flour
1 bunch green onions
½ cup white wine, not too
    dry
1 pint raw mushrooms,
    sliced
1 pound small raw shrimp,
    peeled
1 teaspoon salt
½ teaspoon ground white
    pepper
¼ teaspoon cayenne

Poach the trout:

Pour the water into a wide shallow saucepan. Add the onion, lemon, peppercorns, salt, bay leaves, and thyme. Bring to a boil and reduce to a simmer. Poach the trout filets at a low simmer for 5 minutes or until they are cooked all the way through. Carefully remove the filets from the water and place them on a warm platter with a little of the poaching liquor. Cover and keep warm. Reserve 1½ cups of the poaching liquor, strained.

Make the sauce:

Melt the butter and add the flour. Cook together for 2 minutes and add the green onions, wine, and the reserved poaching liqour. Bring to a boil and add all remaining ingredients, except the trout filets. Reduce heat and simmer for 10 minutes. Adjust seasonings if necessary. Place the trout filets on warm plates and spoon over the Marguery sauce. Serves 6.

VARIATIONS:

The fish can be whatever you have, though I would suggest it be filet. I find that unbone fish becomes a bit tedious in a richly sauced preparation as this is.

NOTE:

The fish should be nice and flaky but not too soft.

TROUT MEUNIERE

Originally a French dish, this recipe has become a most popular dish in New Orleans restaurants.

The *meuniere* is the miller or the man who mills the wheat and grains. Because the mills in France were located on streams where the grindstones were turned by the water it stands to reason that the trout from those streams were prepared with a little freshly ground flour as batter. *Et Voila! Meuniere,* or in the fashion of the miller.

The now classic Louisiana version is generally prepared with an egg batter. Make a batter by combining the half and half, eggs, salt, and pepper. Melt the butter in a large skillet. Dip the trout filets in the batter, dredge in the flour and lay to cook in the hot butter. Cook on both sides until golden brown. Pour the lemon juice over the trout filets, sprinkle with the minced parsley and serve with some of the pan liquid poured over.

1 cup half and half
2 whole eggs
1 teaspoon salt
½ teaspoon white pepper
6 six-ounce skinned trout
    filets
¾ cup flour
3 sticks butter
½ cup lemon juice
2 tablespoons minced
    parsley

VARIATIONS:

You can use just about any fish available for this recipe.

NOTE:

Don't let the batter get too heavy. It should remain light.

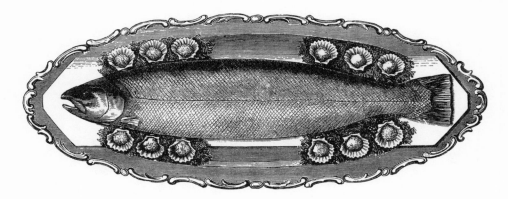

Eggs
and Omelettes

EGGS FLORENTINE

This is one of the grand haute creole dishes in this collection. It is equally as delicious done with trout as a dinner meal (see p. 76).

Make the creamed spinach:

Wash the spinach and discard the tough stem pieces. Chop the leaves. Melt 2 tablespoons butter in a large saucepan and add the spinach. Cover the pot and simmer for about 15 minutes or until the spinach becomes limp.

In a small saucepan melt the butter and blend in the flour. Stir and cook for 2 minutes without coloring the flour. Whisk in 1 cup hot milk. Season with salt and pepper and simmer until thickened. Pour the cream sauce into the spinach, blend together, and simmer for 2 minutes more or until all is well thickened. Rectify seasoning. Set aside and keep warm.

Make the hollandaise:

Put the egg yolks, lemon juice, salt, and cayenne in the top part of a double boiler. Cut the butter sticks in half and add 1 of the 6 pieces to the egg yolk mixture. Heat the water in the bottom of the double boiler without ever letting it come to a boil. Whisk the mixture until the butter is completely melted. Add the next piece. Continue this process until you have used all the butter pieces. Keep whisking over the heat until the sauce has thickened. Remove from heat and continue whisking until the sauce has cooled slightly. Keep warm.

2 ten-ounce bags of fresh spinach
2 tablespoons butter

3 tablespoons butter
3 tablespoons flour
1 cup hot milk
2 teaspoons salt
1 teaspoon pepper

FOR THE HOLLANDAISE:
6 large egg yolks
3 tablespoons lemon juice
1 teaspoon salt
1/4 teaspoon cayenne
3 sticks butter

Water, enough to get a 4-inch depth
1 teaspoon salt
2 tablespoons vinegar
12 large eggs

1/4 cup grated Swiss cheese
1/4 cup grated Parmesan
1/2 cup bread crumbs

Poach the eggs:

Fill a wide shallow saucepan with 4 inches of water. Add the salt and vinegar and bring to a simmer. Break each egg into a tea cup and gently slide the egg into the water. Do this until you have all 12 eggs in the water. Bring back to a simmer and cook for 3 to 4 minutes more. Remove the eggs carefully from the water with a slotted spoon and rest on a towel to drain. Trim the eggs of any unsightly pieces. Keep warm.

Assemble the dish:

Spoon the creamed spinach into 6 individual ovenproof baking dishes. Top each with 2 poached eggs. Spoon over the hollandaise. Blend the bread crumbs and cheeses and sprinkle over the hollandaise. Place in a preheated 400-degree oven for 5 minutes or until the tops begin to brown. Serves 6.

VARIATIONS:

Use any creamed vegetable of your preference to make this dish even more delicious to you personally.

Almost any available filet of fish could be substituted.

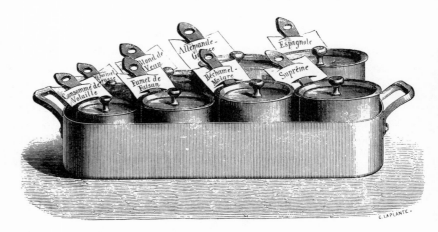

EGGS HUSSARDE

Perhaps it was the french word *husar* for pirate, or the brilliantly colored uniforms of the Hungarian Hussar, the light cavalry of the fifteenth century, that fostered the idea for the name of this richly colored, sauce enrobed concoction. Or even perhaps named after a friend of the family. This dish expanded the concept of the sauced, poached egg by the use of two sauces. It ranks today still as one of the most popular dishes of the Brennan family heritage of classic creations.

MARCHAND DE VIN SAUCE

- 3 tablespoons butter
- 3 tablespoons flour
- 1 onion, minced
- 1 pint fresh mushrooms, minced
- 1 tomato, peeled, seeded and minced
- 1 whole head garlic, peeled and minced (yes, the whole head!)
- 1 rib celery, minced
- 2 tablespoons minced parsley
- 2 bay leaves
- ¼ teaspoon thyme
- 1 cup red wine
- 1 cup beef stock
- 1 teaspoon salt
- ½ teaspoon ground white pepper
- 1 teaspoon sugar

Make the marchand de vin:

Melt the butter and add the flour. Cook together until they begin to color and add the minced onion and mushrooms. Cook together until lightly browned and add all remaining ingredients. Simmer slowly for 45 minutes.

Make the hollandaise:

Put the egg yolks, lemon juice, salt, and cayenne in the top part of a double boiler. Cut the butter sticks in half and add 1 of the 6 pieces to the egg yolk mixture. Heat the water in the bottom of the double boiler without ever letting it come to a boil. Whisk the mixture until the butter is completely melted. Add the next piece. Continue this process until you have used all the butter pieces. Keep whisking over the heat until the sauce has thickened. Remove from heat and continue whisking until the sauce has cooled slightly. Keep warm.

Sauté the ham in butter until the slices are lightly colored. Set aside and keep warm. Sauté the sliced tomatoes in the same butter as the ham. Season with salt and pepper. Set aside and keep warm.

FOR THE HOLLANDAISE:

6 egg yolks

3 tablespoons lemon juice

1 teaspoon salt

¼ teaspoon cayenne

3 sticks butter

1 stick butter

12 three-ounces slices
    smoked ham

3 large tomatoes, sliced
    crosswise in fours

Salt and pepper to taste

12 ½-inch thick rounds of
    stale french bread

Water, enough to fill pan
    to a 4-inch depth

2 teaspoon salt

2 teaspoon vinegar

12 eggs

Paprika

In the same butter (add more if needed) fry the rounds of french bread to make croutons. Set aside.

Poach the eggs:

Fill a wide shallow saucepan with 4 inches of water. Add the salt and vinegar and bring to a simmer.

Break each egg into a tea cup and gently slide the egg into the water. Do this until you have all 12 eggs in the water. Bring back to a simmer and cook for 3 to 4 minutes more. Remove the eggs carefully from the water with a slotted spoon and rest on a towel to drain. Trim the eggs of any unsightly pieces. Keep warm.

Assemble the dish:

Place 2 french bread croutons on each plate and top each with a slice of ham. Spoon some marchand de vin sauce over the ham and top with a slice of tomato. Put a poached egg on each tomato slice and spoon over the hollandaise. Sprinkle with paprika for color. Serve 2 per person. Serves 6.

VARIATIONS:

French bread is not crucial here. English Muffins or Holland Rusks or simply toast will do.

NOTE:

There are a lot of steps to this dish and it may seem unnecessarily complicated, but if you want the real thing you have to go the full route. This dish is popular because of its interesting complexities.

EGGS SAINT DENIS

Juchereau de Saint Denis was a native of Canada, educated in Paris, who came to Louisiana during the early years of French domination to seek his fortune. He became quite influential over the Indians of Louisiana and was often called upon to handle government affairs in this area.

His patron saint, Saint Denis, died a Christian martyr by decapitation, and is the patron saint of headaches. It is said that when Saint Denis's head was cut off, he got up, picked up his head and walked away.

This preparation is rather unusual in that the eggs are poached in hot oil, rather than water. This actually fries them in a round form. They should not be overcooked.

1 stick butter
1 cup minced chicken livers
⅓ cup minced ham
1 onion, chopped
2 toes garlic, minced
4 tablespoons flour
½ teaspoon thyme
½ cup sherry
2 cups chicken stock
Salt and pepper to taste

1 stick butter
12 three-ounce slices of
    ham
12 ½-inch thick rounds of
    stale french bread
Deep fat, enough for
    3-inch depth
12 eggs

Prepare the sauce:

Melt the butter in a heavy saucepan and sauté the minced chicken livers, ham, onions and garlic. When the onions begin to color, add the flour. Cook together until all is nicely browned. Add the thyme, sherry, and chicken stock. Bring to a simmer and season to taste with salt and pepper. Simmer slowly for 20 minutes. Keep warm.

To sauté the ham, melt the butter in a heavy wide skillet and sauté the slices briefly. Set them aside and keep warm. Fry the french bread rounds in the butter, turning once, until lightly browned and crisp. Keep warm with the ham.

Poach the eggs in deep fat at 350 degrees just as you would in water. Break the eggs into a cup and slip them one by one into the heated oil. Turn them in the oil so that they form an oval shape. Cook just long enough for the whites to firm up but the yolks to remain runny, about 2 minutes. Carefully drain them on paper and trim off any stringy pieces. Keep warm.

Assemble the dish:

Put 2 fried croutons on each plate. Top each with a piece of ham and an egg. Spoon over the Saint Denis sauce. Serves 6.

VARIATIONS:

You can use this method of poaching in oil for the eggs in any dish calling for regular poached eggs. It makes an interesting difference in the textures of the finished product.

NOTE:

Don't overcook the eggs. Even though the dish is still quite good with the eggs cooked all the way through, I prefer to have the yolks uncooked as in poached egg dishes.

EGGS SARDOU

New Orleans has long been known for its elaborate breakfast menus and dishes, even before the now popular "brunch" had come into existence. The first haute Creole poached egg dish in our cookery was invented by Jules Alciatore at Antoine's. The dish was Eggs Sardou, named for the then famous French playwright Victorien Sardou, to whom the dish was served at a breakfast at Antoine's in 1908.

6 quarts water, or enough
    to cover the artichokes
2 lemons, halved
6 tablespoons salt
2 tablespoons olive oil
12 small artichokes

HOLLANDAISE SAUCE
8 large eggyolks
4 tablespoons lemon juice
1 teaspoon salt
¼ teaspoon cayenne
4 sticks butter, or 1 pound

Water, enough to fill your
    saucepan 4 inches
1 teaspoon salt
2 tablespoons vinegar
12 large eggs

24 anchovy filets
12 slices truffle

Prepare the artichokes:

Put the water in a large pot. Squeeze the juice in and add the lemons to the water. Add the salt and olive oil. Bring to a boil. Put the artichokes into the water and boil for 30 to 45 minutes or until the stems are tender. Remove the artichokes from the water to drain. Hold the artichokes with a towel and cut off the stems, and remove the leaves and the chokes. Put the hearts on a warm plate in a little of their cooking liquor and keep warm.

Make the hollandaise:

Put the egg yolks, lemon juice, salt, and cayenne in the top part of a double boiler. Cut the butter sticks in half and add 1 of the 8 pieces to the egg yolk mixture. Heat the water in the bottom of the double boiler without ever letting it come to a boil. Whisk the mixture until the butter is completely melted. Add the next piece. Continue this process until you have used all the butter pieces. Keep whisking over the heat until the sauce has thickened. Remove from heat and continue whisking until the sauce has cooled slightly. Keep warm.

Poach the eggs:

Fill a wide shallow saucepan with 4 inches of water. Add the salt and vinegar and bring to a simmer. Break each egg into a tea cup and gently slide the egg into the water. Do this until you have all 12 eggs in the water. Bring back to a simmer and cook for 3 to 4 minutes more. Remove the eggs carefully from the water with a slotted spoon and rest on a towel to drain. Trim the eggs of any unsightly pieces. Keep warm.

Assemble and serve:

Place two warm artichoke hearts on each warm plate. Crisscross two anchovy filets over each heart and top with a poached egg. Spoon the hollandaise over the eggs and garnish the top of each with a slice of truffle. Serve immediately. Serves 6.

VARIATIONS:

It is not uncommon to find this dish employing spinach— boiled or creamed—in place of the anchovy filets. Some prefer this alternate to the original recipe here.

You might want to use a slice of black olive in place of the truffle. The visual effect of the black dot is quite effective.

NOTE:

Who keeps truffles around the house anymore? I know I don't. But do use a slice of black olive. It really does add a nice colorful contrast against the yellow of the hollandaise.

I haven't made hollandaise in a double boiler at home since I acquired a blender years ago. If you haven't made blender hollandaise you absolutely must try it this time. You can't go wrong!

Blender Hollandaise:

Same ingredients as given.

Melt the butter in a saucepan to an almost boil. Put all the other ingredients into the blender and give it a hit on low for ten seconds. Now turn on the blender on low and remove the top, and slowly pour the hot butter in a thin stream into the blender until it is all in the mixture. Voila! Instant perfect hollandaise.

CROUTON OMELETTE

This is one of the first omelettes served in the original Begue's restaurant in the old French Market to the purveyors there. It was inexpensive to prepare but tasty, with interesting texture differences.

Cut up the stale french bread into ½-inch cubes. Melt the butter in a wide skillet and fry the croutons, stirring them around until they are browned on all sides. Remove and set aside.

For each omelette beat 3 eggs together with ½ teaspoon salt and ½ teaspoon pepper, just enough to blend the yolks and whites. Heat 2 tablespoons butter in an omelette pan. Mix about ½ cup of the croutons with the mixed eggs and pour into the pan. Lift the sides of the omelette while cooking to let the uncooked eggs flow underneath. When the omelette is almost cooked fold it into thirds and into the corner of the pan to finish cooking. Turn out onto a plate and keep warm. Continue this process until all the omelettes are made. Serves 6.

10-inch piece stale french
    bread
1½ sticks butter
1½ dozen eggs
Salt
Pepper
1½ sticks melted butter

NOTE:

The sheer simplicity of the recipe leads me to take it as it is and not change much about it.

Be sure the croutons are nicely browned on all sides. If the croutons are not properly prepared the omelette will suffer.

CREOLE OMELETTE

The sauce used here is the basic sauce in all of Creole cookery. We use it elsewhere in this collection in the recipes for Shrimp Creole and Chicken Creole.

The Omelette Creole makes a marvelous dish for both breakfast and lunch.

½ stick butter
3 onions, chopped
2 bell peppers, seeded and
    chopped
5 tomatoes, skinned, seeded
    and chopped
¼ teaspoon thyme
2 bay leaves
1 teaspoon paprika
2 toes garlic, minced
2 tablespoons minced
    parsley
Salt and pepper to taste
½ teaspoon cayenne

1 pint fresh mushrooms,
    sliced
2 tablespoons butter
1 eight-ounce can peas,
    drained
3 dozen eggs
2 teaspoons salt, or to taste
1 teaspoon pepper, or to
    taste
1½ sticks melted butter

Make the sauce:

Melt the butter in a wide skillet and sauté the onions and bell peppers until they become limp. Add the tomatoes, thyme, bay leaves, paprika, garlic and parsley. Season to taste with salt, pepper, and cayenne. Simmer for 20 minutes or until most of the liquid is cooked out. Adjust seasoning. Keep warm.

Cook the omelettes:

Sauté the mushrooms briefly in the butter and put them in a mixing bowl. Add the green peas. Break the eggs into the same bowl and season with 2 teaspoons salt and 1 teaspoon pepper, or to taste. Beat the mixture together lightly. Put 2 tablespoons melted butter in the small skillet or omelette pan and ladle in some of the egg mixture (the equivalent of 3 eggs with some of the mushrooms and peas). Cook on a low fire until the omelette is cooked all the way through.

Do not fold this omelette—it is served flat. When the omelette is cooked, turn it out onto a plate, bottom-side up, and spoon over some of the Creole sauce. This recipe makes 6 omelettes.

VARIATIONS:

Since this is the most important dish in Creole cookery I have included the complete recipes for Shrimp Creole and Chicken Creole in this volume.

Notes:

I feel strongly that the Creole sauce should never be over-cooked. All the vegetables should remain distinguishable in the final product, not cooked together into a puree, such as in a tomato sauce.

Chicken,
Duck, and Squab

63.

64.

65.

66.

CAJUN FRIED CHICKEN

The Cajuns were the French-Canadians who came to settle in Louisiana. They, for the most part, survived as hunters, trappers and fishermen. Many of their descendants today still work the same areas. One of the notable aspects of the style of cookery that they developed is its spicyness. Spicy fried chicken has long been a favorite in our home.

It is interesting to see this dish being welcomed with such relish on a national level.

Cut up the chickens for frying. Blend the salt, pepper, and cayenne together. Rub down the chicken pieces with the salt and pepper mix and put in a covered container in the refrigerator for several hours to give the pepper time to penetrate the chicken. Rub the seasoned chicken pieces with flour. Heat the oil to 350 degrees and add the chicken. Do not crowd the pan. Fry on each side until golden brown and the chicken is cooked completely through, about 10 minutes. Drain on paper. Serves 6 to 8.

2 frying chickens
3 tablespoons salt
2 tablespoons black pepper
1 tablespoon cayenne
2 cups flour

VARIATIONS:

Too hot for you? Use less pepper and cayenne.

Shrimp, oysters and crayfish can all be cooked this way.

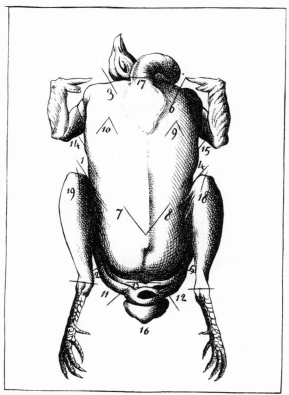

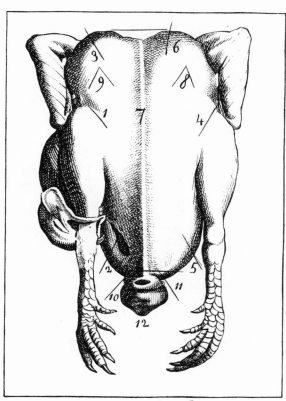

Le Chapon   *La Poularde*

CHICKEN BONNE FEMME

This is one of those "house" dishes that we have at Antoine's that came from the Cajun country with the cooks. Traditionally, it was not on the menu, but it was so good that I finally did put it on and the dish is now available to anyone.

Put the bacon into a large frying pan and onto the fire. Begin rendering the fat.

Rub the chicken pieces with the 2 tablespoons salt and 1 tablespoon pepper. Dredge the chicken in the flour.

When the fat is rendered from the bacon and the bacon is just beginning to crisp, remove the bacon pieces from the fat and set them aside on a plate. Add the peanut oil to the pan with the bacon grease and heat. Add the chicken pieces to the fat and fry until golden and completely cooked. Remove the chicken and set aside. Add the onions and potatoes to the hot fat and cook them together until the potatoes are cooked through, but not mushy. Don't break up the potato slices when cooking. When the potatoes are done, add the minced garlic, the bacon, and the cooked chicken pieces.

Cover and simmer together on a low fire for about ten minutes more. Add the chopped parsley and serve. Serves 6 to 8.

1 pound bacon, cut crosswise into ½-inch pieces
2 chickens, approximately 3 pounds each, cut into frying pieces
1½ cups flour
2 tablespoons salt
1 tablespoon black pepper
1 cup oil, preferably peanut
4 large potatoes, skin on, cut crosswise into ⅛-inch chips
2 large white onions, chopped
4 cloves garlic, minced
2 tablespoons chopped parsley
Salt and pepper to taste

VARIATIONS:

You might want to add more garlic for a stronger taste. The potatoes could be cut into cubes instead of slices.

NOTE:

Don't overcook the potatoes. The dish is lovelier and more interesting when the potatoes are properly cooked and not all stuck together or broken into a mush.

CREOLE CHICKEN

We banter around the terms Creole and Cajun as though the difference between the two is understood by everyone. In fact, you are very likely to get many differing opinions about the definitions of the two terms. The Creoles were and are the descendants of the French and Spanish who came to Louisiana. The Cajuns are the descendants of the French Acadians who came from Canada (Acadia) to settle in Louisiana. For the most part, the Creoles were the city dwellers and plantation owners and the Cajuns were the hunters and trappers in the country.

This recipe uses the sauce that is basic to Creole cookery.

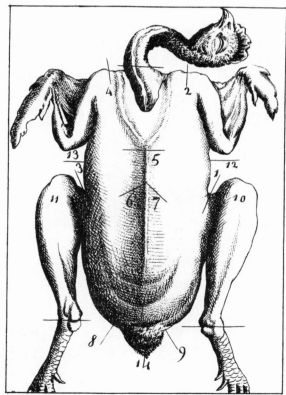

La Poule bouillie.

Cut up the chicken as for frying. Blend the salt, pepper and flour together and rub the chicken pieces with the mixture. Heat the peanut oil in a heavy wide skillet and brown the chicken pieces. Set aside.

Add the chopped onions and bell peppers and sauté them until the onions are transparent. Add all the remaining ingredients. Simmer together slowly for 10 minutes.

Add the cooked chicken pieces, cover and simmer slowly for 20 minutes.

Cook the rice:

Bring 4 cups water to a boil with 2 teaspoons salt and 2 tablespoons butter. Add 2 cups rice and simmer slowly for 20 minutes.

Serve the chicken and Creole Sauce on a plate accompanied with the hot cooked rice. Serves 6 to 8.

VARIATIONS:

Already we have included the recipe for Shrimp Creole which is the most popular variation of this dish. These two are the standards.

NOTE:

Don't overcook the Creole sauce. This is not an Italian tomato sauce and should not be cooked down to a complete mush. The vegetables should remain distinguishable in both taste and texture.

2 chickens
1 tablespoon salt
1 tablespoon pepper
½ cup flour
½ cup peanut oil

3 onions, chopped
2 bell peppers, seeded and chopped
5 tomatoes, chopped
¼ teaspoon thyme
2 bay leaves
1 teaspoon paprika
2 cloves garlic
2 tablespoons minced parsley
2 teaspoons salt or to taste
½ teaspoon black pepper or to taste
½ teaspoon cayenne or to taste
4 cups water
2 teaspoons salt
2 tablespoons butter
2 cups uncooked rice

CHICKEN ROCHAMBEAU

Jean Baptiste Donatien de Vimeur, Comte de Rochambeau, was born in France in 1725. He became a general in the French army and helped in the American Revolution by leading the French forces against the British at Yorktown, Virginia, in 1781. Together his troops and the American forces defeated the British in that battle.

Years later he barely escaped the guillotine during the Reign of Terror and was eventually given a pension by Napoleon. Rochambeau died in Thore, France in 1807.

Antoine Alciatore, who invented this dish, named many of his greatest creations after men of history. His original version of Chicken Rochambeau was served with a thick slice of roast turkey instead of the half chicken. During my tenure at Antoine's I changed the dish from turkey to chicken.

Rub the chickens inside and out with 2 tablespoons salt and 1 tablespoon black pepper. Roast in a preheated 350-degree oven for 1½ hours or until completely cooked. Remove the chickens from the oven and cool long enough to handle. Split the chickens in half and remove the breast bones. Keep warm. While the chickens are roasting, prepare the two sauces.

Brown Rochambeau Sauce:

Sauté the chopped onions in the butter until they begin to color. Add 3 tablespoons flour and cook together until browned. Blend in the vinegar, sugar, and chicken stock. Season with salt and pepper. Simmer slowly for 20 minutes.

Bearnaise sauce:

Put the minced onion, parsley, tarragon leaves and ¼ cup tarragon vinegar in the top of a double boiler and completely reduce the liquid. Cool slightly. Whisk in the egg yolks and cook, stirring constantly until the mixture thickens. Blend in the melted butter a little at a time. Add the lemon juice, salt and cayenne. Remove from the heat and continue whisking until the Bearnaise Sauce has cooled slightly. Do not let the sauce get too hot during cooking or it will separate.

Assemble the dish:

Grill the ham slices lightly in a heavy skillet and arrange them on dinner plates.

Ladle some of the Brown Rochambeau Sauce over each slice of ham. Lay a half roasted chicken over each ham slice and top the chicken with Bearnaise Sauce. Serves 6.

3 small chickens
2 tablespoons salt
1 tablespoon pepper

FOR THE ROCHAMBEAU SAUCE:

1 onion chopped
4 tablespoons butter
3 tablespoons flour
¼ cup vinegar
2 tablespoons sugar
2 cups chicken stock
Salt and pepper to taste

FOR THE BEARNAISE SAUCE:

½ onion, minced
2 tablespoons minced parsley
2 tablespoons minced tarragon leaves
¼ cup tarragon vinegar
6 egg yolks
3 sticks butter
1 tablespoon lemon juice
½ teaspoon salt
½ teaspoon cayenne

6 four-ounce slices smoked ham

VARIATIONS:

You can use cornish hen or duck for this preparation. In both cases you should serve ½ per person.

NOTE:

I prefer the chicken roasted but this recipe can be followed with boiled chicken.

This dish is quite rich so the chickens should not be too large.

GARLIC CHICKEN

The sheer simplicity and absolute deliciousness of garlic and chicken make it a dish that is often served at my house.

The best restaurant in our area for dishes with garlic is Mosca's Restaurant where the food is scrumptuous.

Cut the chicken into pieces as for frying. Rub the pieces with the salt and pepper. Heat the butter in a heavy skillet and sauté the chicken. When the pieces are nearly cooked add the garlic, parsley and white wine.

Cover the pan and simmer slowly for 15 minutes. Adjust seasoning. Serves 6 to 8.

2 chickens
1 tablespoon salt
2 teaspoons ground black
    pepper
3 sticks butter
2 whole heads garlic, peeled
    and chopped
½ cup chopped parsley
½ cup white wine

VARIATIONS:

This preparation lends itself beautifully to smaller birds like cornish hens and quail.

You could use a good light olive oil instead of the butter if you prefer.

NOTE:

Be sure to serve some good hot bread for sopping up the sauce.

ROAST DUCKLING
WITH APPLES AND ONIONS

Duck dishes are ever popular in Louisiana due to the great abundance of wild game. The state motto which can be seen on every license plate is "Sportman's Paradise." Again we see ducks cooked as many ways as chicken. All of my recipes are interchangeable.

The hunters are the fortunate ones because it is they who have the best wild ducks. But if you don't have wild ducks you can prepare any duck recipe with those fat ducklings you find in any large grocery. These ducklings make a delicious meal but they must be properly cooked.

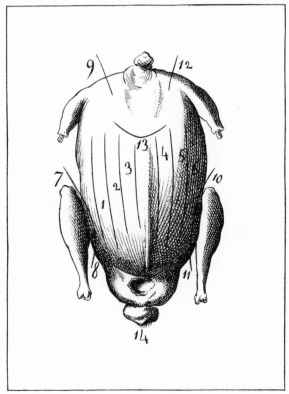

Le Canard sauvage et domestique

Prick the ducklings over all fatty areas to allow the fat to drain as the ducks roast. Rub the ducklings inside and out with the salt and pepper. Set aside.

Cut the apples into quarters, removing the stems and seeds. Peel and quarter the onions. Put the apples and onions together in a bowl and sprinkle them with salt and pepper. Stuff the ducklings with the apples and onions and put the remaining apples and onions in the roasting pan. Put the ducklings in the roasting pan and into a preheated 350-degree oven for approximately 2½ hours or until the ducks are completely cooked. Baste the apples and onions during cooking to keep them moist. Serve the ducklings quartered with the apples and onions as the vegetable. Serves 8.

2 four-pound ducklings
1 tablespoon salt
1 teaspoon pepper
8 apples
8 onions
Salt and pepper

VARIATIONS:

Wild and domestic ducks, chicken, cornish hen or goose would all be good prepared in this manner.

NOTE:

Cook the birds slowly to eliminate excess fat and assure tenderness.

Only the fat ducklings should be pricked before cooking and all the birds but the duckling should be basted.

If you use wild ducks, wrap the breasts with strips of bacon to keep them moist and to add another delicious element of flavor.

ROAST DUCK WITH OYSTER STUFFING

A festive preparation that works equally as well with all available poultry, duck, chicken, cornish hen or turkey.

FOR THE OYSTER STUFFING:
¼ pound bacon, chopped
½ stick butter
Liver, heart and gizzard from the ducks, minced
1 large onion, chopped
1 bunch green onions, chopped
2 tablespoons chopped parsley
2 ribs celery, chopped
4 toes garlic, minced
3 bay leaves
¼ teaspoon thyme
2 cups raw oysters, chopped
½ teaspoon salt, or to taste
1 teaspoon pepper, or to taste
4 cups stale french bread crumbs
1 cup chicken stock

2 four-pound ducklings
1 tablespoon salt
1 teaspoon pepper

Make the oyster stuffing:

Put the chopped bacon in a heavy skillet to render the fat. Add ½ stick butter and the minced liver, gizzard and heart. Add the chopped onion, green onions, parsley, celery, garlic, bay leaves and thyme. Cook together until the vegetables brown somewhat. Add the chopped oysters, pepper, and ½ teaspoon salt. Continue cooking for 2 minutes more and then add the bread crumbs. Blend all ingredients well, adding enough chicken stock to supply wetness to hold the mixture together. Adjust seasonings and cook for 2 minutes more without drying the stuffing out too much. Set aside.

Roast the duck:

Rub the ducklings inside and out with salt and pepper. Prick the skin with a small knife so that the fat will drain during the roasting. Stuff the ducklings with the oyster stuffing. Place them breast up in a shallow roasting pan. Roast in a preheated 350-degree oven for about 2½ hours, or until they are completely done.

When the ducklings are cooked, remove them from the roasting pan to a warm platter and put them back in a low oven to keep warm.

Make the gravy:

Add the chicken stock to the roasting pan with the drippings and heat on the stove while stirring and scraping the pan. When the pan drippings are blended into the stock, remove about ¼ cup and mix it with the cornstarch. Return this to the pan and mix well. Bring to a boil.

When gravy thickens pour it into a serving bowl and send it to the table with the stuffed ducklings.

FOR THE GRAVY:
pan drippings
1 cup chicken stock
2 teaspoons cornstarch
salt and pepper to taste

VARIATIONS:

This recipe works well with all poultry available in the market. Change the cooking times of the birds according to the roasting instructions on the wrapper: turkey, cornish hen, or duckling.

NOTE:

I think I prefer this preparation with domestic birds to wild birds because the wild birds have already enough flavor to carry themselves through most preparations, whereas the domestic birds can use the oyster flavor for enrichment.

DUCK SAUCE PIQUANTE

It was terribly cold that day, and still the darkest hour of the day, morning, about 3:30 A.M. We had made it to the camp from New Orleans in a reasonable amount of time and we were now all getting ready to breakfast before the first hunt of the season. Our friend, Henry, was cooking for us then. He would later be our guide to the ponds for the hunt, after we had had breakfast. Henry was a bachelor, forty-years old, and had acquired quite a skill at the stove. It seemed to me now that all the men in our group who were from the Cajun country in Louisiana knew how to cook. They were less macho and a bit more sensitive as a group than many of their contemporaries, and they lived as their fathers and grandfathers lived. In fact, Henry's house was still without electricity in the late fifties. Imagine! The gas for the heaters and the stove was trucked out and stored in a large tank that sat at the side of the battered old cypress cottage.

This morning at the camp there was promise for a special day. It was always that way on the first day of the season. A ritual of sorts ensued: there was lots of bantering and laughing among the hunters who were fresh out of the city and away from the worries of their lives. Henry was occupied with the preparation of the breakfast as all of the others checked and rechecked their shotguns, and made sure all was in working order for the main event of the day, the hunt. I was more interested in what Henry was doing. The smells that filled the small rough cabin were unfamiliar to me, and seemed incongruous in this simple cabin in the swamp. The bisquits came out first and the group gathered at the large round table to begin the meal. Conversation died down as the food was presented. We sat and ate the bisquits, big and soft and buttery, with lots of Louisiana strawberry preserves that tasted like they had been cooked the same day. Henry cautioned us not to fill up on the bisquits.

"Why don't ya'll clear the table so I can serve you breakfast?" We made a clearing in the middle of the table as Henry walked over from the stove with the black pot that had been there since we arrived that morning.

"Man, Man!" the hunters exclaimed as the top of the pot was lifted and the smells from within filled the entire room. "What a treat, Henry." they said as they dug in and passed plates of the luscious halves of duck in the red-brown sauce. As we ate the duck, there were reverent murmers of gratitude from the men. I savored the moment. This was a dish almost legendary in the annals of Louisiana cookery but one that I had not yet experienced. The perfumes of the sauce were decidedly different from our normal fare. There was a blending of vinegar and the brown roux and the bit of tomato, all combined to pique the sense of smell and taste. And pique it did.

Henry's theory in serving ducks to hunters before the hunt had something to do with his belief that the hunters needed a bit of the prey to hunt their best.

Duck Sauce Piquante has as many variations as cooks, as do most of the great dishes in Louisiana cookery. Mine is the version that I have best been able to approximate from that cold wet morning in camp twenty years ago.

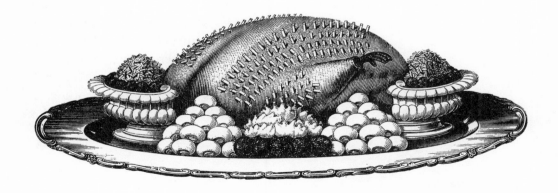

2 four-pound ducklings
Salt
Pepper
½ cup duck fat, reserved
    from the roasting pan
½ cup flour
1 large onion, chopped fine
4 cloves garlic, minced
2 large tomatoes, skinned,
    seeded and chopped
½ cup red wine vinegar
3 cups duck stock (reserved
    pan juices with enough
    chicken stock or water
    to make 3 cups)
½ teaspoon cayenne
½ teaspoon white pepper
½ teaspoon black pepper
2 teaspoons salt
3 bay leaves
½ teaspoon thyme
½ bunch green onions,
    chopped fine

Roast the duck:

Since wild duck is not available to all of us, I will describe the method for roasting those fat ducklings that are found in the market.

Rub the washed, defrosted ducklings with salt and pepper. Prick the fatty areas of the duck so that the fat will drain during the roasting time. Place the ducklings breast up in a shallow open roasting pan. Roast in a preheated 325-degree oven for 2 hours, or 30 minutes per pound (5 pound ducklings 2½ hours, 6 pound ducklings 3 hours). Do not baste during roasting; you want the fat to drain. When the ducklings are cooked, remove them from the pan and cool slightly, then cut them into pieces as for frying. Pour the pan drippings into a glass measuring cup and let the fat come to the top. Drain off the fat and reserve ½ cup and all the duck juices.

Make the sauce:

Pour the ¼ cup reserved duck fat from the roasting pan into a saucepan. Add the flour and cook and stir until it gets a nice medium brown color. This is the roux. Add the onions to the roux and continue cooking until they have browned. Add all remaining ingredients, except the green onions, bring to a boil and turn down to a simmer. Cook for 15 to 20 minutes at a simmer, or until the sauce acquires a nice consistency. Add the chopped green onions and simmer for 3 minutes more. Adjust seasoning. The taste should have a nice bit of both vinegar and pepper.

Assemble and simmer:

Put the duckling pieces into a pan, pour on the sauce piquante and simmer together for 30 minutes or until the duck is very tender. Serves 6 to 8.

VARIATIONS:

If you use wild duck you may want to simply halve the ducks and serve ½ duck per person. In this case roast the duck by your own recipe.

I have often prepared this dish by removing the meat from the carcass after roasting and cooking it down like a stew. When I do this I like to serve the Duck Sauce Piquante spooned over the wild rice with raisins and pecans recipe included in this collection.

At times I have removed the skin from the duck before roasting, cut the skin into ½ inch squares, fried them in fat, seasoned them with salt, and sprinkled the crisp "cracklins" over the finished duck dish. This is a superb garnish and adds a wonderful dimension to the recipe.

NOTE:

Lighten up on the pepper if it is too much for you.

SQUAB PARADIS

On one of his annual trips to France with his father, Jules Alciatore, Roy found a dish that he particularly liked and he pursuaded the chef to give him the recipe. Some years after his father's death, Roy, as proprietor of Antoine's, was on a hunting trip with some friends in a camp in Paradis, Louisiana. Roy decided to present this dish to his fellow hunters for dinner. It was so well received that he put it on the menu at Antoine's and called it Squab Paradis.

6 squabs (4- to 5-week-old
    baby pigeon)
Salt
Pepper
Butter

8 strips bacon, chopped
3 tablespoons flour
1 bunch chopped green
    onions
1 stalk celery, minced
1½ cups chicken stock
½ cup sherry
3 tablespoons red currant
    jelly
Salt to taste
½ teaspoon pepper, or to
    taste
1 cup seedless green grapes

Roast the squabs:

Wash and dry the squabs and rub them inside and out with salt, pepper, and butter. Put the squabs in a shallow roasting pan and into a preheated 325-degree oven for 45 minutes. Remove from the oven and set aside.

Make the sauce:

Make the paradis sauce while the squabs are roasting. In a saucepan, add the chopped bacon and render the grease without letting the bacon begin to crisp. Add the flour and cook together for about two minutes. Add the green onions, the celery, the chicken stock, the sherry and the currant jelly. Blend well and bring to a boil. Lower to a simmer.

Season with the salt and pepper and add the grapes. Continue simmering together until the grapes are somewhat softened, about 10 minutes. Adjust seasoning if necessary. Put the roasted squabs in a large saucepan and pour the paradis sauce over them. Cover and simmer gently for 15 minutes. Serves 6.

VARIATIONS:

Even though we use squab (young pigeon) for this recipe, it is delightful with ducks, chickens or cornish hens.

If you don't have fresh seedless grapes, you can use canned green seedless grapes.

NOTE:

This dish is quite sweet and should be recognized as such.

Meat

BOILED BEEF (BOUILLI)

Interestingly, the brisket used in this dish was at one time discarded after the cooking and the broth was used for stocks and soups. The Creoles weren't ones to discard any good product and soon devised many appetizing ways to serve the *bouilli*. This preparation became a standard in the old restaurants and can still be found in a few today. It makes a great meat dish for the family.

Put the beef brisket in a soup pot. Add the onions, celery, garlic, parsley, bay leaves, thyme, salt and whole black peppercorns. Cover with water and bring to a boil. Turn down the heat and simmer slowly for 2½ to 3 hours or until the brisket is very tender.

Make a horseradish sauce by blending the horseradish, creole mustard and ketchup. Chill. When the brisket is ready, remove it from the cooking water. Drain and slice it to serve. Serve slices with the sauce on the side. Serves 6 to 8.

4 pounds beef brisket
2 onions, sliced
2 ribs celery, chopped
4 toes garlic, mashed
3 sprigs parsley
3 bay leaves
½ teaspoon thyme
2 tablespoons salt
12 whole black peppercorns
Water

½ cup horseradish
½ cup creole mustard
1 cup ketchup

VARIATIONS:

You could use any tough cut of beef in this recipe.

NOTE:

There is another sauce that was once served with the *bouilli* that was a blend of half cream sauce and half horseradish.

The best restaurant in New Orleans to go for a true *bouilli* or boiled beef served in the traditional fashion is Tujague's Restaurant.

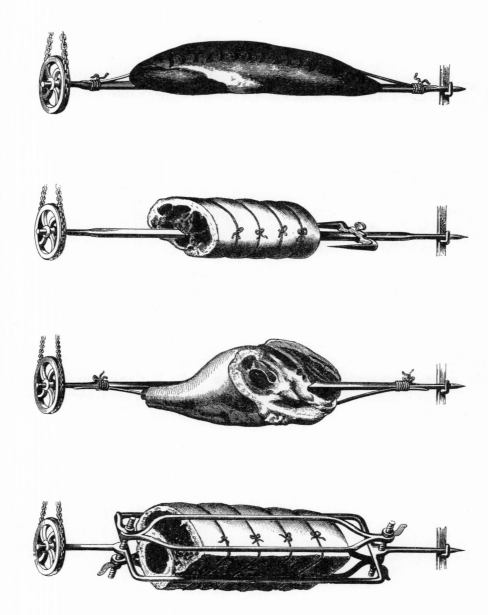

BEEF FILET WITH MARCHAND DE VIN SAUCE

The sauce, Marchand de Vin, is a classic of French cuisine. It was a sauce invented in the markets by the wine merchants *les marchands des vins* using their own wines. The classic French version employs *moëlle* or marrow as a principle ingredient and does not use as much garlic. This version is the one that New Orleanians have loved for many years.

Make the sauce:

Melt the butter and add the flour. Cook together until they begin to color and add the minced onions and minced mushrooms. Cook all together until brown. Add all remaining sauce ingredients and simmer slowly for 45 minutes. Keep warm.

Cook the filets:

Blend the oil with the salt and pepper and rub into the steaks. Cook the filets in a hot skillet to desired doneness. Remove to dinner plates and serve with the Marchand de Vin spooned over. Serves 6.

VARIATIONS:

Any steak cut could be prepared this way accompanied with the Marchand de Vin.

NOTE:

Many people prefer to have their sauces served on the side so they can taste it before it covers the meat. This way each person can use as much of the sauce as they want.

3 tablespoons butter
3 tablespoons flour
1 onion, minced
1 pint fresh mushrooms, minced
1 tomato, peeled, seeded, and minced
1 whole head garlic, peeled and minced
1 rib celery, minced
2 tablespoons minced parsley
2 bay leaves
¼ teaspoon thyme
1 cup red wine
1 cup beef stock
1 teaspoon salt
½ teaspoon ground black pepper

¼ cup oil
2 teaspoons salt
1 teaspoon pepper

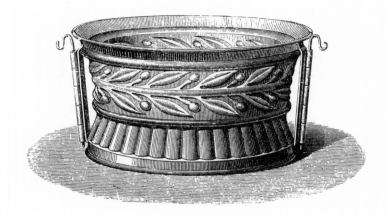

DAUBE GLACÉE

Daube Glacée is another of those dishes that fall into the category of Haute Creole. Fashioned after Boeuf a la Mode, it has taken on Creole characteristics. It is a wonderful summer dish, when you want a light meal, and winter, when it can grace the table as a most attractive course in a meal.

Very much like a hog's head cheese with a lighter, subtler flavor.

Heat the oil in a large wide skillet and sear the beef round, pig's feet, and salt pork. Brown on all sides. Add the onions, carrots, celery, garlic, parsley, thyme, bay leaves, and cloves. Pour in the sherry and beef stock. Season with salt, ground black pepper, and cayenne. Bring to a boil and turn down to a slow simmer. Cover the pot and simmer for 2½ to 3 hours or until the meat is very tender.

Remove the pig's feet and beef round from the pot. Remove the bones and cut up the meat. Return the meat to the pot. Check seasoning. Simmer for 30 minutes more. Take a cup of the simmering liquid from the pot and dissolve the gelatin into it. Pour this back into the pot and stir. Turn off the heat and let cool slightly. Ladle the mixture into a 2-quart loaf pan. Cover the pan with film and chill in the refrigerator for 4 hours or so before serving. Unmold the Daube Glacee onto a platter, slice and serve. Serves 6 to 8.

VARIATIONS:

You may want to omit the pig's feet. The reason they were included originally was not only for flavor but also, and perhaps more important, for the gelatin they contain necessary to mold the glacée. With the gelatin included in this recipe you can omit the pig's feet.

NOTE:

You don't see this dish offered much anymore. It probably has to do with the length of time that it takes to prepare. It's fun though, and a wonderful offering to bring to a friend's home for a big dinner.

I make sandwiches with the leftovers and they are delicious.

You can mold the glacée in muffin cups for individual servings.

¼ cup oil

3 pounds heavy veal or beef round

2 pig's feet, split

½ pound salt pork

2 onions, chopped

2 carrots, sliced

1 rib celery, chopped

2 cloves garlic, minced

2 sprigs parsley, chopped

½ teaspoon thyme

3 bay leaves

6 whole cloves

1 cup sherry

1½ quarts beef stock or water

1 teaspoon salt, or to taste

1 teaspoon ground black pepper

½ teaspoon cayenne

1 packet gelatin

GRILLADES AND GRITS

Grillades and Grits is the traditional and necessary dish to begin any midnight supper or Sunday morning brunch. We use veal or beef round, pounded out, seasoned, and smothered to a tender texture and served in their own cooking juices with grits. This is a dish that you still find prepared in many homes, especially when their are numerous guests to feed.

2½ pounds veal or beef round
¼ cup oil
2 tablespoons flour
1 large onion, chopped
2 tomatoes, chopped
1 bell pepper, chopped
3 cloves garlic, minced
2 tablespoons minced parsley
2 bay leaves
2 teaspoons salt
1 teaspoon black pepper
2 cups beef stock
6 servings grits, cooked according to package directions

Pound the veal or beef rounds and cut into 2 × 3-inch pieces. Heat the oil in a wide heavy skillet and brown the meat. Remove the meat from the skillet and hold aside. Add the flour to the skillet and cook while stirring until you get a brown roux. Add the onions and cook for 5 minutes more. Add all remaining ingredients including the meat and simmer together for 1 hour or until the meat is tender and the sauce is thickened. Adjust seasonings.

Make the grits:

While the grillades are simmering prepare 6 servings of grits according to package directions. Keep warm. Spoon the grits onto warm plates and ladle the grillades alongside. Serves 6.

VARIATIONS:

This dish can be made with better cuts of meat if you prefer, but the original purpose was to make a wonderful meal out of a cut that was tough to begin with.

The grits could be enhanced by adding some grated cheddar cheese and maybe a touch of minced garlic.

Some cooks do not use tomato sauce.

NOTE:

This is a great buffet dish. It can be cooked and kept for hours in a chafing pan and still maintain it's quality.

SWEETBREADS FINANCIERE

The sweetbread can be either the thymus or the pancreas of a calf or a lamb. It has a strong flavor reminiscent of liver and is usually reserved for the gourmet.

The classic French *Sauce Financiere*, would be a demi-glace (brown sauce base), flavored with truffle, where our Haute Creole version is a brown sherry sauce garnished with chicken livers and olives. The dish has strong rich flavors good for a cold winter's eve, and is worthy of a good red Bordeaux.

Blanch the sweetbreads:

Salt the water and bring it to a boil. Drop in the sweet-breads and boil for 2 minutes. Remove them from the water and cut them into 1-inch pieces. Melt the butter and sauté the sweetbreads seasoned with a little salt and pepper until they are lightly colored. Set aside.

Make the sauce:

Put the butter and bacon in a saucepan to heat. Add the chicken livers and sauté them until they are cooked and lightly colored. Remove the chicken livers, cut them up and set aside. Add the flour, chopped onions, green onions, and carrots. Cook together until you have achieved a nice brown color. Add the garlic, parsley, celery, thyme, bay leaves, the tomato pulp and the tomato paste.

Add the sherry and the beef stock. Season with the salt and pepper, add the halved olives and chicken livers and simmer for 20 minutes.

Add the sweetbreads to the sauce and simmer for 20 minutes more. Serves 6.

VARIATIONS:

This dish is also served as a sauce for grilled beef steak. In this case you would want to cut the sweetbreads, chicken livers and olives into smaller pieces.

2 tablespoons salt
2 quarts water
2 pounds cleaned
    sweetbreads
½ stick butter
½ teaspoon salt
½ teaspoon pepper

¼ pound bacon cut into
    1-inch pieces
½ pound chicken livers
4 tablespoons flour
1 onion chopped fine
½ bunch green onions,
    chopped fine
1 carrot chopped fine
2 cloves garlic, minced
2 tablespoons minced
    parsley
1 rib celery, minced
½ teaspoon thyme
3 bay leaves
1 large tomato, skinned,
    seeded, and minced
2 tablespoons tomato paste
½ cup sherry
2 cups beef stock
Salt and pepper to taste
½ cup pitted green olives,
    halved

TRIPE CREOLE

This is a dish that was once quite popular in Louisiana but has since lost its standing as a favorite. I think it is probably because not as many children are exposed to this type of dish because so few families are butchering their own meat and using all of the parts. It was, however, a principal dish on the menus of the city's restaurants for many years and can still be found on occasion. Arnaud's Restaurant has an excellent tripe dish that is the best available in the city of New Orleans.

This rendition is not unlike Tripe a La Mode de Caen with only a few local differences.

My first encounter with the dish was at Antoine's as a child. I always went for the most exotic sounding dishes available. Even though its lack of present popularity has caused it to be removed from the Antoine's menu I still enjoy it whenever I pay a visit to Arnaud's.

Put 2½ quarts water in a deep saucepan. Add the onion, lemon, peppercorns, cloves, vinegar, salt, and cayenne. Bring to a boil and add the tripe. Boil for 2 hours or until the tripe is tender. Remove the tripe, dry it, and cut it into 1 × 2-inch strips. Set aside.

In another pan melt the butter and add the flour. Cook together long enough to get a light brown-colored roux. Add the chopped onions and cook together until the onions begin to color. Add all remaining ingredients except the tripe. Simmer, covered, for 20 minutes. Add the tripe and simmer for another hour. Adjust seasoning if necessary. Ladle into bowls and serve.

VARIATIONS:

If tripe is not a favored meat in your house you can make an absolutely delicious stew with beef round steak.

NOTE:

I love this dish but am very cautious about serving it. Be sure your guests are up to it before you spend too much time on a dish that might not be appreciated.

2½ quarts water
1 sliced onion
1 sliced lemon
12 whole black peppercorns
12 whole cloves
¼ cup vinegar
2 tablespoons salt
1 teaspoon cayenne
2½ pounds tripe
4 tablespoons butter
2 tablespoons flour
2 large onions, chopped
½ cup minced ham
2 large tomatoes
1 small bell pepper
1 rib celery
2 tablespoons minced
   parsley
1 teaspoon thyme
3 bay leaves
3 cloves garlic, minced
½ teaspoon ground allspice
2 tablespoons tomato paste
½ cup red wine
1½ cups beef stock
1 teaspoon salt, or to taste
½ teaspoon black pepper
½ teaspoon cayenne

VEAL ROLLS STUFFED WITH OYSTERS AND SAUSAGE

There was a time when veal was the less expensive meat available. There are many New Orleanians who grew up never having a beef steak until they were out of the family home and could afford to have one themselves. It seems ironic now that good veal is more expensive than beef.

In those times there were many ways to serve veal devised to give variety to its preparation. Veal rolls was an excellent way to prepare veal because the veal did not have to be high quality to produce a good dish. This does not mean to say that good quality will not yield a better dish.

Veal rolls can be stuffed with any sort of dressing that you prefer.

1 pound hot pork sausage, without casing
½ stick butter
1 onion, chopped
1 bunch green onions, chopped
2 tablespoons chopped parsley
2 ribs celery, chopped
4 toes garlic, minced
3 bay leaves
¼ teaspoon thyme
1 pint raw oysters
½ teaspoon salt or to taste
1 teaspoon pepper or to taste

Make the dressing:

Break up the pork sausage and put it in a heavy skillet with the butter to render the fat and cook the sausage. When the sausage begins to color add the chopped onion, green onions, celery, garlic, parsley, bay leaves, and thyme. Cook together until the vegetables begin to brown.

Add the chopped oysters and their liquor and cook for 3 minutes. Blend in the bread crumbs and the beef stock. Season with salt and pepper. Cook together for 2 minutes without drying out the dressing too much. Set aside.

Prepare the veal:

Remove the bones and cut the rounds crosswise into 3 pieces each. Pound the pieces out with a rolling pin or meat hammer and season them with salt and pepper. Spoon the dressing onto the centers of the veal pieces and roll the meat around the dressing. Tie them with string or secure with toothpicks to keep them from opening up during cooking. Put the veal rolls in a greased covered baking pan and bake in a 350-degree oven for 30 minutes. Remove the cover, baste the veal rolls and bake for 10 or 15 minutes more. Serves 6.

3 cups crumbled stale
    french bread crumbs
1 cup beef stock
2 two-pound veal round
    steak
Salt
Pepper

VARIATIONS:

Both shrimp and crayfish in place of the oysters in the stuffing make excellent substitutes. If you want, you can exclude the sausage.

NOTE:

Cook the veal long enough for it to be tender. Don't forget to remove the string or toothpicks before serving.

LIVER AND ONIONS

This is a great family favorite that can also be found in many of the restaurants. Even those who aren't keen on liver are likely to find this preparation delicious.

½ cup flour
1 teaspoon pepper
2 teaspoons salt
2½ pounds calf or beef
    liver
1 stick butter
½ pound bacon, cut
    crosswise into
    ½-inch strips.
6 toes garlic, chopped
6 onions, sliced
    paper thin
2 cups beef stock

Combine the flour, pepper, and salt and rub it onto the liver slices. Set aside. In a large heavy skillet, melt the butter and add the bacon. When the bacon becomes translucent but has not yet begun to color add the liver. Sauté on both sides until nicely colored. Add chopped garlic and onions and continue sautéeing until the onions are translucent. Add the beef stock. Simmer together for 20 minutes or until the liver is tender. Serves 6.

VARIATIONS:

You might want to go even a little further with this preparation and add some fresh mushrooms and a little sherry.

NOTE:

This is a dish that I wake up some mornings craving. It is delicious and the odor of onions, garlic, and bacon cooking together is irresistible.

Red Beans and Rice,
Jambalaya,
and Stuffed
Vegetable Dishes

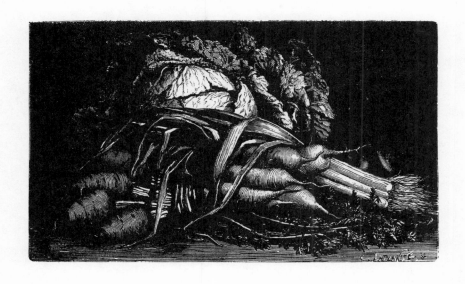

BELL PEPPERS
STUFFED WITH GROUND BEEF

These make a good entrée or can be split and served as a side course. Some of the best in the city are at Chez Hélène, where chef owner Austin Leslie has made his mark with excellent homestyle Creole food.

Remove the stems and seeds from the bell peppers and set them aside. Melt the butter in a wide skillet. Add the onions, celery, parsley and garlic. Add the ground beef and sauté together until the beef is completely cooked and the vegetables are lightly browned. Add the bread crumbs and season with salt and pepper. Remove from heat and let cool slightly.

Work the eggs into the stuffing. Adjust seasoning if necessary. Spoon the stuffing into the prepared bell peppers and place them in a shallow baking dish.

Bake in a preheated 350-degree oven for 30 minutes or until the the bell pepper shells are tender. Serves 6.

6 bell peppers
½ cup peanut oil
1 large onion, chopped
2 ribs celery, chopped
3 tablespoons minced
   parsley
3 toes garlic, minced
2 pounds ground beef
4 cups bread crumbs
3 eggs
2 teaspoons salt, or to taste
1 teaspoon pepper, or to
   taste

VARIATIONS:

Ground pork, veal or lamb can all be used in place of the beef.

Shrimp and crabmeat also make excellent stuffings.

The addition of Parmesan cheese and a tomato sauce are popular.

NOTE:

If the stuffing becomes all together too dry, add a little beef stock or water.

Stuffed peppers are good single meals. I serve very little else when I serve these.

BLACKEYED PEAS AND PICKLED PIGS' TAILS

We have dishes that employ almost every bean available. The blackeyed pea is actually a bean and this preparation is second only to red beans and rice.

Blanch the tails:

In a heavy saucepan, add 2 tablespoons salt to 1½ quarts water (or enough water to cover the pigs' tails) and bring to a boil. Add the pigs' tails and boil for 2 minutes. Remove the pigs' tails from the water and chop into pieces 1-inch thick. Set aside.

Heat the oil in a large heavy pot and add the chopped onions and blanched pigs' tail pieces. Sauté together until all begins to color. Add the garlic, bay leaves and water. Season with salt and pepper and simmer slowly for 1½ to 2 hours or until the beans are completely cooked and the sauce is thick.

While the beans are simmering prepare the rice.

Put 4 cups water in a pot to boil. Add 1 teaspoon salt and 1 tablespoon butter. Add 2 cups rice, cover and simmer for 20 minutes or until the rice is cooked and all the liquid is absorbed. Serve the peas and pigs' tails ladled over the rice. Serves 6 to 8.

VARIATIONS:

Of course you don't have to use pigs' tails! Use ham or sausage if you prefer.

NOTE:

Blackeyed peas, red beans, white beans and navy beans can all be cooked in similar fashion.

2 tablespoons salt
1½ quarts water
1 pound pickled pigs' tails
    (about 2)
¼ cup oil
1 large onion, chopped
2 large toes garlic, minced
3 bay leaves
6 cups water
2 teaspoons salt
1 teaspoon ground black
    pepper

4 cups water
1 teaspoon salt
1 tablespoon butter
2 cups rice

RED BEANS AND RICE

It's Monday afternoon, three o'clock. The bell rings and class is over. It has taken all day to get back into the schoolday and out of the weekend, tromping through the swamps, swimming in Lake Pontchartrain, collecting bones of small animals from beneath the wild blackberry bushes, and catching a few prize snakes for our collection at home in the city. My mother was pretty good about that, the snakes that is. The grammar school was only a few blocks away, and a pleasant walk down the oak-lined avenue. The branches of the immense oaks formed a ceiling over the street and kept it cool, even on the hottest days of summer. With the knapsack packed and slung up on my back, I would start the trek home, with a feeling of apprehension for having to begin my homework on my arrival.

Reaching the gate of the wrought iron fence that surrounded our front yard, I would look up at the top of the gate where, "Sisters of Mercy" was written in wrought iron letters. When the old convent for the Sisters of our school was torn down, their iron fence made its way to our yard. It was a beautiful fence and still stands there today, sans "Sisters of Mercy" signage.

We always used the back door—the front door was reserved for guests. That was fine with us, though. The back door entered directly into the kitchen, and every Monday afternoon as I entered I would suddenly know that it was Red Beans and Rice day! The kitchen was filled with the comforting smell of something sure and regular, something on which you could depend, even in those grammar school years of fast growing and constant change.

Monday is washday. Red Beans and Rice are traditionally served on washday. It makes sense: the wash takes hours to do and the beans take hours to cook. They could both be done at the same time. Besides, after the feast that would usually grace the family table on Sunday, it was necessary to balance out the grocery budget with something less costly.

In our refrigerator there was always a ham. Mostly this was used for the sandwiches we would make all week and bring to school. Or perhaps the ham would be baked and it would be our Sunday dinner. By Monday, the hambone and its week's memory would be put in the pot with the Red Beans to both flavor and romance the dish.

Now, homework didn't seem such a chore knowing that at six thirty we would sit down to one of our favorite meals.

That meal would give me the strength to get through the week to Friday afternoon at three when life would begin again.

Wash the beans and put them in a heavy soup pot with 2 quarts water. Bring the water to a boil and turn down to a simmer. Continue simmering for one hour. Add all remaining ingredients except the cooked rice. Simmer for another hour and a half or so, or until the beans have become tender and have made their own thick sauce. Stir occasionally to prevent any scorching on the bottom. Adjust seasoning.

To serve, ladle over one cup rice per portion. Serves 6 to 8.

1 pound red kidney beans
2 quarts water
1 large onion, chopped
1 bell pepper, seeded and chopped
1 bunch green onions, chopped
3 bay leaves
¼ teaspoon thyme leaves
2 cloves garlic, minced
2 tablespoons minced parsley
1 pound pickled pork, cut into 1-inch pieces
1 hambone (optional)
1 tablespoon salt, or to taste
1 teaspoon black pepper, or to taste
¼ teaspoon cayenne pepper, or to taste
6 to 8 cups hot cooked rice

VARIATIONS:

Ham, salt pork, smoked sausage, andouille sausage or kielbasa could be used in place of the pickled pork or hambone.

NOTE:

I usually mash about a cup of the cooked red beans and blend them back into the rest to make a thicker sauce of the liquid in the pot.

JAMBALAYA WITH ANDOUILLE SAUSAGE

Jambalaya, like gumbo, can be made with just about any combination of ingredients that you prefer. It is an area of cooking as much as it is a single dish. It counts as one of the most important dishes in all of Louisiana cookery.

½ cup peanut oil
1 large onion, chopped
1½ pounds sliced
    andouille sausage,
    cut crosswise into
    ½-inch slices
1 bell pepper, chopped
1 large tomato, chopped
2 cloves garlic, minced
3 bay leaves
¼ teaspoon thyme
2 tablespoons minced
    parsley
1½ quarts beef stock
1 teaspoon black pepper
½ teaspoon cayenne
3 cups rice
Salt to taste

In a large saucepan or skillet, heat the oil and sauté the chopped onions. When the onions begin to color, add the sausage slices and the chopped bell pepper. Sauté together until the sausage is cooked and the bell pepper begins to color. Add the chopped tomato, the minced garlic, the bay leaves, thyme, parsley and hot beef stock. Add 1 teaspoon black pepper and ½ teaspoon cayenne. Bring to a boil. Add the rice, bring to a boil again and reduce to a simmer. Cover and simmer for about 25 minutes or until all the liquid is absorbed and the rice is somewhat dry and not too sticky. Adjust seasonings.

Spoon onto serving dishes and serve. Serves 6

VARIATIONS:

The number of possible variations of this dish is endless. Everybody has his own special combination. Keep your principle ingredient (in this case andouille sausage) from 1½ to 2 pounds but make it anything you have or want— ham and shrimp, duck and pork sausage, oysters, alligator. Almost all variations should contain some sort of hot or smoked sausage to give the jambalaya a good country flavor. There should always be some kind of Louisiana hot sauce accompanying this dish for the real fire eaters. The stock could be chicken stock, or fish/shellfish stock for jambalaya with seafood.

NOTE:

The jambalaya could be concocted from already cooked rice with the addition of the remaining ingredients.

STUFFED EGGPLANT

Stuffed eggplant is our most common and most popular stuffed vegetable dish. It can be served as an entrée or as a side or vegetable course. And eggplants have the flexibility of being able to be stuffed with almost anything your heart desires.

Every Louisiana cook I know thinks he or she makes the best stuffed eggplant, and the best gumbo, and the best red beans, because what each of us grows up with always seems to be the best and proper way to prepare these dishes.

You can stuff an eggplant with just about anything you want. There are some garnishes that are more traditional than others—ham, shrimp, crabmeat, or any combination thereof. I like to use them all together. That can get a bit costly, but it is well worth the expense.

This seems a terribly long list of ingredients, but it all goes together rather quickly.

Cut the eggplants in half lengthwise, put them in a large pot, and pour in enough water to cover them completely. Add two tablespoons of salt and bring the water to a rolling boil. Turn down to a simmer, and continue cooking for approximately 30 minutes, or until the meat of the eggplant is soft. Carefully remove the eggplants from the water without tearing the skins. Put them in a collander to drain and cool. When they are cool enough to handle, remove the meat from the skins using a soup spoon. Again be very careful that you don't damage the skins; they become the shell that must be stuffed. Place the shells in a buttered baking dish. Chop the eggplant meat and set aside.

Put the diced bacon into a large frying pan and heat long enough to render the fat. When the fat is rendered from the bacon, but the bacon has not begun to crisp, add the butter. When the butter is completely melted and hot, add the following ingredients: chopped onion, green onion, bell pepper, and celery. Cook these together until they become limp. Add the chopped eggplant meat. Stir well together and add the garlic, parsley, salt, pepper, paprika, thyme, and bay leaves.

Blend all together and add the shrimp and smoked ham. Add 1 cup bread crumbs and remove from the heat. When the mixture is cooled a bit, blend in the eggs and ½ cup of the Parmesan cheese. Spoon the mixture into the eggplant shells in the baking dish. Mix ¼ cup Parmesan with ½ cup bread crumbs and sprinkle the mixture over the stuffed eggplants.

Place the stuffed eggplants into a preheated 375-degree oven, and bake for about 25 minutes, or until the tops are golden brown.

Remove and serve. Serves 6.

3 large eggplants
Water
2 tablespoons salt
¼ pound bacon, diced
1 stick butter
2 large onions, chopped
1 bunch green onions, chopped
½ medium-sized bell pepper, finely chopped
2 stalks celery, finely chopped
4 cloves garlic, minced
2 tablespoons minced parsley
1 teaspoon salt
1 teaspoon black pepper
½ teaspoon paprika
½ teaspoon thyme
3 bay leaves
1 pound small shelled shrimp, preferably uncooked
1 pound smoked ham, cut into ½-inch cubes
1½ cups bread crumbs (reserve ½ cup for topping)
2 eggs, beaten
¾ cup Parmesan cheese (reserve ¼ cup for topping)

VARIATIONS:

The shrimp and ham could be replaced with almost anything you want. Most commonly we use crabmeat. There is no reason you couldn't use scallops or oysters or even lobster. You decide.

NOTE:

If the shrimp or whatever other product you use for the stuffing are not cooked, you might want to be sure that you cook them completely in the eggplant mixture in the pan before you add the bread crumbs. This will allow any liquids from the product to be released now so you can achieve a proper stuffing texture, and also assure you that that product will be fully cooked.

This is a good dish to make for just 2 people and wrap the other 4 stuffed eggplants tightly and individually in a clear wrap and freeze, for future meals when you want something wonderful but don't have the time to prepare it.

This dish almost becomes a complete meal. A small salad is really all you would want to add to round out the dinner.

CRABMEAT STUFFED MIRLITONS

Mirlitons are not as easily available as eggplant but can be stuffed as many different ways.

It is also known as the vegetable pear or the chayote.

Boil the mirlitons in enough salted water to cover them completely for 45 minutes to one hour or long enough so that they are easily pierced with the blade of a sharp knife. Remove, cool and cut the mirlitons in half lengthwise. Discard the seed. Scrape out the meat with a spoon leaving ¼- to ½-inch thickness in the shell. Be careful not to cut through the skins during this process. Chop the meat and set aside.

Melt the butter and sauté the onions and green onions until they are limp. Add the chopped mirliton meat, the garlic, parsley, thyme, salt, black pepper, and cayenne and simmer together for five minutes. Fold in the crabmeat and bread crumbs and simmer for 5 minutes more.

Remove from heat, cool slightly and blend in the egg. Adjust seasoning if necessary. If the stuffing is too dry and will not hold together add another egg.

Spoon the mixture into the mirliton shells and sprinkle with the remaining ½ cup bread crumbs. Bake in a pre-heated 350-degree oven for 30 minutes or until the tops are browned. Serves 6.

3 large mirlitons
2 tablespoons salt
Water

1 stick butter
1 medium onion, chopped
½ bunch green onions, chopped
2 cloves garlic, minced
2 tablespoons parsley, minced
¼ teaspoon thyme
1 teaspoon salt
½ teaspoon black pepper
½ teaspoon cayenne
½ pound crabmeat
1 cup bread crumbs, ¾ cup for stuffing and ¼ cup for topping
1 large egg, beaten

VARIATIONS:

Mirlitons can be stuffed many different ways. Some of the most popular are with shrimp and ham or with ground beef or pork. Simply substitute the same amount of your stuffing ingredient as the crabmeat.

Note:

This makes an excellent side dish or entrée.

BOUDIN

Boudin is a classic of Louisiana cookery that is not as difficult to prepare as it would seem.

Traditionally there are two types of boudin: white and red. The red boudin is actually a blood pudding or sausage whereas the white boudin is a rice and pork or veal stuffed sausage. The French word *boudin* means pudding.

Red boudin is rarely ever seen. Its commercial production was banned years back because of the possible health hazards of the pork or calf blood in the recipe.

Mince the pork or veal and put it in a pot with the chopped onions, green onions, garlic, parsley, thyme, bay leaves, salt, pepper, and cayenne. Add just enough water to meet the level of the ingredients. Bring to a boil and simmer for 10 minutes. Put the ingredients into a bowl and stir in the cooked rice. Adjust seasonings if necessary. Tie the 4 sausage casings at one end and stuff them with the mixture. Twist each 20-inch length into three equal lengths. Tie open end.

The boudin can be cooked covered in a little water, grilled or pan fried in a little butter. Cut the sausages and serve 2 to each person. Serves 6.

2 pounds lean pork or veal
2 onions, chopped
½ bunch chopped green onions
2 toes garlic, minced
½ bunch chopped parsley
½ teaspoon thyme
2 bay leaves
1 tablespoon salt, or to taste
1 teaspoon ground white pepper, or to taste
1 teaspoon cayenne, or to taste
2 cups water
3 cups cooked rice (package recipe)
4 twenty-inch long cleaned sausage casings

VARIATIONS:

This dish is a good one to learn because once you have mastered its preparation you can use almost anything in place of the pork or veal. Some of the most popular are chicken, shrimp, crabmeat, and crayfish.

Bread is a traditional but not as good replacement for the rice.

NOTE:

This is a great dish to make and it freezes well. Many people cut the casing off of the boudin before eating it.

Salads

GREEN SALAD WITH VINAIGRETTE DRESSING

This is the classic green salad served by the Creoles. It is rarely found now because of its complexity of greens. Most often it is done with only some of the greens listed here.

This recipe has been used at Antoine's for many years and is called "Antoine's Salad."

Prepare the dressing:

Combine the vinegar, salt, pepper, and powdered mustard. Slowly whisk in the olive oil. Set aside while you prepare the greens.

Prepare the greens:

Wash and dry all the greens. Remove all the undesirable parts and discard. Break all the large leaves into 2 inch pieces. Toss the greens together with the vinaigrette dressing. Serves 6 to 8.

VARIATIONS:

All of the greens are not necessary. You can get a good simple salad with any combination of the greens listed.
If you have a preferred dressing use it.

NOTE:

This salad is wonderful because of the various tastes of the greens. It tastes far more interesting than it looks.

¼ cup vinegar
1 teaspoon salt
1 teaspoon ground white
    pepper
½ teaspoon powdered
    mustard
¾ cup olive oil

1 small head bibb lettuce
1 small head romaine
    lettuce
2 Belgian endive
1 bunch watercress

ANCHOVY SALAD

This salad is one of the first salads served in the homes of the Creoles and in the old restaurants of the French Market. Salted fish and anchovies were frequently used in the days before refrigeration.

When the Creoles served anchovies they considered them to be very elegant because they were imported. Madame Begue and Madame Antoine both highlighted anchovies on their menus.

When I was spending a summer in the little town of Agay, on the French Riviera near St. Tropez, I first discovered freshly salted anchovies. What a marvel I thought they were. Already I was a fan of the regular tinned-in-oil brands, but never had I seen them packed in salt. I bought a container of them and asked the shopkeeper how to eat them. He told me that first you must rinse them under cold running water to remove the salt. Then with your fingers you pull the filets from the still remaining skeleton of the anchovy. I went back to villa where I was staying and to the kitchen sink and went through the prescribed process. I ate the first filet and knew immediately that I had never tasted an anchovy with the flavor of this one. I was delighted.

The friends with whom I was staying soon caught up to me at the kitchen sink and we all ate the anchovies.

Since that time I occasionally reward myself with a large tin of salt-packed anchovies available in the Italian markets in the city. Salt-packed tins are the closest available product to the freshly salted anchovies in the south of France.

Make the vinaigrette dressing:

In a bowl combine the vinegar, salt, pepper, powdered mustard, and olive oil. Whisk together until slightly thickened.

Make the salad:

Shell the four hard-boiled eggs and rough chop them. Strain the oil from the can of anchovies and dice the filets. Chop the romaine and the bibb lettuce. In a salad bowl, toss the chopped lettuce, chopped eggs and the diced anchovies.

When they are well mixed toss them with the vinaigrette dressing. Serve on cold salad plates. Serves 6 to 8.

⅓ cup vinegar
½ teaspoon salt
¼ teaspoon white pepper
½ teaspoon powdered
    mustard
1 cup light olive oil
4 hard-boiled eggs
1 small tin anchovy filets
1 small head romaine
    lettuce
1 small head bibb lettuce

VARIATIONS:

This salad is served today in the existing old restaurants without the addition of the boiled eggs. This preparation is also quite good.

NOTE:

This dish is very salty and that must be considered before serving it. I am a heavy salt user and consider this one of my favorite salads.

BEET AND RED ONION SALAD

One of the great joys of growing up in New Orleans with an excellent Creole cook in the kitchen was dinner at home. This was the only time of the day that the entire family was expected to be together. It was the time that all discussions were heard, requests made, pleas for the use of the car presented. More often than not, there would be a few extras, neighbors and friends, who would end up at the table with us, and it was not uncommon for the table to be set for ten or so on almost any evening. And there were always a few dogs lounging around under the table, ready to help out any child that could not "clean his plate."

Our cook was the best: Nancy Madison. Proud Creole of Color who felt that we were as much her children as anyone else's. On any subject we would get our parents' opinion and then get Nancy's opinion to be sure our parents were correct. We were expected to finish our meals, even if that night's menu happened to include Possum Stew!

Leave it to Nancy to balance out the meal with something we all liked, something like beet and red onion salad. This is a good and different salad. The dressing is as simple as can be, the crunchy red onions give it all the zip it needs, and the beets round out the taste with their sweetness.

Years have passed. Nancy is now cooking for the angels in heaven and the kids are all adults. The other night I prepared a beet and red onion salad. The tastes flooded my mind with memories of those evening meals at the family table, and of Nancy Madison.

"Roy, why are you sniffling?" Mimi asked me as we finished our plates.

"It's just the onions, Mimi," I answered.

Add the salt to the water and bring to a boil. Add the beets making sure they are completely covered by the water. If not, add more water. Boil the beets for 30 to 45 minutes or until tender. Remove them and chill in ice water. Slice the onions and chill them in the refrigerator. In a large salad bowl, whisk together the vinegar, oil, salt, and pepper.

Dry, peel, and slice the cold beets. Put the beets and onions in the salad bowl and toss together in the dressing. Serves 6 to 8.

2 quarts water
2 tablespoons salt
6 large fresh beets (or canned beets)
3 large red onions
¼ cup red wine vinegar
¾ cup olive oil
½ teaspoon salt
¼ teaspoon white pepper

VARIATIONS:

No, the onions don't absolutely have to be red, but red onions are sweeter and less pungent than other onions and are better for this salad. Plus the color makes the salad more attractive.

The beets can be canned. They are not often available fresh. If you use canned beets, do not cook them.

ARTICHOKES WITH GARLIC MAYONNAISE (AIOLI)

This is one of those dishes that has come in my family to be related to Good Friday. As a traditional fasting day in Catholic ritual the dishes served on this day didn't contain meats. This did not mean however that the dishes were drab. The Creoles are not ones to suffer with bad food. This dish is absolutely delicious and one that we have more often than on "fasting" days.

3 tablespoons salt
2 tablespoons oil
2 bay leaves
Water, enough to cover
    the artichokes
6 artichokes
2 eggs
1 teaspoon salt
½ teaspoon pepper
2 tablespoons lemon juice
6 toes garlic, pressed to a
    purée
1½ cups light olive oil

Boil the artichokes:

Add the salt, oil, and bay leaves to the water and bring to a boil. Add the artichokes and simmer for about 45 minutes or until the stems are tender and the leaves can be easily removed from the artichoke. Drain and chill in the refrigerator.

Make the aioli:

Beat the eggs with the salt, pepper, lemon juice and pressed garlic. Slowly whisk in the oil and continue whisking until the sauce has emulsified, or reached the proper consistency. Cover and refrigerate. Serve one artichoke per person with the aioli for dipping. Serves 6.

VARIATIONS:

You might want to try this dish with any mayonnaise you want: dill, lemon, anchovy.

NOTE:

Homemade mayonnaise makes the sauce something special, but it is not absolutely necessary provided you flavor it properly.

CREOLE TOMATO SALAD

I have yet to taste a tomato as delicious as a vine-ripened Louisiana Creole tomato. The sweetness of the taste and the thick fleshy texture of the meat make these tomatoes the best. There is also a richness of tomato taste in the Creole that I have not found in another tomato.

These tomatoes are grown only in Louisiana and are an actual variety, whereas many of the vegetables grown in Louisiana are called Creole although there is really no distinguishable difference from other varieties.

Raw with just a sprinkling of salt is a perfect way to eat a ripe Creole tomato, but for mealtimes this salad is delightful.

In a bowl whisk together the tarragon vinegar, thyme, salt, and pepper. Whisk the olive oil into the seasoned vinegar and pour it over the salad. Wash and remove the stems from 4 large ripe Creole tomatoes. Slice the tomatoes crosswise into ½-inch slices. Divide up the slices onto 6 salad plates. Sprinkle the chopped green onions over the tomatoes and pour over the dressing. Serve chilled. Serves 6.

¼ cup tarragon vinegar
½ teaspoon thyme
1 teaspoon salt
½ teaspoon pepper
¾ cup olive oil
4 large Creole tomatoes
½ bunch green onions,
      chopped

VARIATIONS:

If you don't have Creole tomatoes, use the best, ripe tomatoes that you can find.

The vinegar in the dressing does not have to be tarragon. White, cider, or wine vinegar can be used

NOTE:

It really is the Creole tomato that makes this salad. Other tomatoes can be used and even though the salad will be good it will not be the same as with real Creoles.

CAULIFLOWER SALAD WITH CAPERS

There were many Sunday afternoon lunches spent at the table in my grandmother's home on Napoleon Avenue. I remember distinctly upon entering the house being hit by the welcoming odor of lamb roasting and cauliflower boiling mixed with the soothing smells of old books and freshly polished furniture. The menu was for the most part always the same: lamb, string beans, and a cold salad of cooked cauliflower with a caper vinaigrette salad. We all loved the meal and no one ever asked for a change.

⅓ cup vinegar
½ teaspoon powdered mustard
1 teaspoon salt
½ teaspoon ground pepper
1 teaspoon sugar
1 cup olive oil
2 small cauliflower heads
2 tablespoons salt
2 quarts water or enough to cover
¾ cup vinegar

Make the dressing:

In a mixing bowl blend the vinegar, powdered mustard, salt, pepper and sugar. Whisk in the olive oil. Add the capers and set aside.

Boil the cauliflower:

Wash the cauliflower and break into branches. Discard the hard stem. Add the salt to the water and bring to a rolling boil. Add the vinegar and the cauliflower. Boil for about 5 minutes, just enough to cook them somewhat so that they are still crisp to the bite. Drain, cover and chill in the refrigerator.

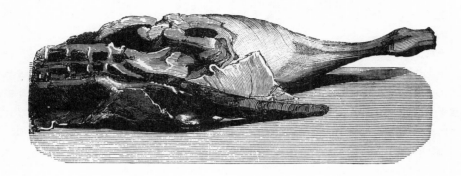

Assemble the dish:

When ready to serve, divide the chilled, cooked cauliflow-
erets onto salad plates and spoon over the dressing with
capers. Serves 6 to 8.

VARIATIONS:

Broccoli and Jerusalem artichokes can be used in place of
cauliflower.

NOTES:

Don't overcook the cauliflower. You may want to steam it
rather than boil it. There should be a bite left to the
texture.

HEAD OF LETTUCE SALAD WITH ONION AND ROQUEFORT DRESSING

One of the wonderful neighborhood restaurants uptown is Charlie's Steakhouse. It was a place where you could bring the whole family. And the steaks were some of the best that I have ever eaten to this day. Along with the steaks we always had wonderful, thinly sliced fried onion rings and a salad of a slice of head lettuce with roquefort and onion dressing. This salad is one that has been around for a long time and can still be found in many of the older restaurants in town.

Make the onions and roquefort dressing:

Slice 1 large onion into paper thin slices. Place in a bowl. In another bowl blend the vinegar, salt, pepper and oil. Crumble the roquefort into the mixture and work together until the dressing is creamy. Pour the dressing over the onions and chill.

Make the salad:

Take 1 large head of iceberg lettuce and cut it crosswise into 6 slices. Place each slice on a chilled salad plate and spoon over the onion and roquefort dressing. Serves 6.

VARIATIONS:

You could omit the onions if this combination is too strong for you.

The salad could be made with chopped lettuce, but it would lose some of its character.

Any lettuce can be used in place of the iceberg lettuce.

NOTE:

The onion should be sliced as thinly as possible. They should be limp and fold into the dressing.

1 large white onion
¼ cup vinegar
1½ teaspoon salt
½ teaspoon pepper
¾ cup olive oil
1 cup crumbled roquefort
1 large head iceberg lettuce, washed

Vegetables

BRABANT POTATOES

We grew up having brabant potatoes the way most kids have french fries. The butter sauce and the crisp brown edges give them added dimension, a more sophisticated taste.

Wash and peel the potatoes and cut them into ½-inch cubes. Keep them in cold water. Melt the butter in a saucepan. Dry the potatoes and sauté them in the butter until they are golden brown and cooked completely through, about 5 minutes. Sprinkle with parsley and serve. Serves 6.

3 large ripe potatoes
2 sticks butter
1 teaspoon salt
½ cup chopped parsley

VARIATIONS:

A touch of minced garlic and freshly ground black pepper in the potatoes is delicious.

NOTE:

This dish can be used as a part of many others. You may sauté the potatoes with other vegetables like green peas for a nice change. Or sauté them with onion and bacon and serve them over a grilled breast of chicken.

BRUSSELS SPROUTS AU GRATIN

Just as it looks, the Brussels sprout is a small cabbage and a member of the mustard family. Brussels sprouts are a popular vegetable in Louisiana cookery.

1½ quarts water, or enough to cover the sprouts
1 tablespoon salt
1 quart Brussels sprouts, washed
3 tablespoons butter
3 tablespoons flour
1½ cups half and half, heated
1 teaspoon salt, or to taste
½ teaspoon white pepper
1/16 teaspoon nutmeg, or a pinch
½ cup grated Swiss cheese
½ cup bread crumbs

Add the salt to the water and bring to a boil. Add the washed Brussels sprouts and bring to a boil again. Cover and continue cooking for 10 to twelve minutes, or until the sprouts are tender. Remove them from the water and drain.

Make the sauce:

Melt the butter in a small saucepan and blend in the flour. Stir and cook together for 2 minutes. Whisk in the hot half and half. Season with the salt, white pepper, and nutmeg. Let simmer for a minute. Blend in the grated cheese and keep warm.

Assemble the dish:

Butter an ovenproof baking dish. Cut the Brussels sprouts in half and lay them, open side up in the baking dish. Pour the hot sauce over the sprouts and sprinkle with bread crumbs.

Bake the sprouts in a preheated 325-degree oven for about 30 minutes or until the top is browned. Serves 6.

VARIATIONS:

Add a little cayenne, say ¼ teaspoon. Sauté ¼ pound
chopped bacon with 1 small chopped onion and add it to
the sauce just before you add the cheese.

NOTE:

If the sauce becomes too thick, add some of the water in
which you cooked the Brussels sprouts to thin it out. Don't
overcook the sprouts.

CANDIED YAMS

Although yams are actually a variety of tuber distinct from the sweet potato, most Louisianians refer to all varieties of sweet potatoes as yams. In this recipe, any sweet potato or yam will suffice.

3 large sweet potatoes
salt
water
1 cup brown sugar
2 large lemons, juiced
½ teaspoon salt

Boil the sweet potatoes in enough salted water to cover them completely. Boil only long enough for the potatoes to become tender enough to easily pierce with a fork. Remove the potatoes from the water, dry and let them cool enough to handle. Peel the potatoes and cut them into eighths and lay them in a baking dish.

Make the syrup:

Combine the sugar, lemon juice, and salt in a small saucepan and heat until the sugar is melted. Pour the syrup over the potatoes and bake in a preheated 350-degree oven for 45 minutes. Turn the potatoes in the syrup several times while baking. Serves 6.

VARIATIONS:

Any variety of sweet potato or yam will do nicely for this recipe.

A dash of cinnamon and a shot of rum add tremendously to the flavor.

NOTE:

This recipe always recalls holiday dinners such as Christmas, Thanksgiving, and Easter. Candied yams are certainly good and simple enough to have more often.

CREAMED SPINACH

We never seemed to have a problem getting the kids at our house to eat their spinach. I used to wonder why so many people claim to dislike it. Perhaps this recipe is the reason spinach has always been so popular in our family.

Wash the spinach and discard the tough stem pieces. Chop the leaves. Melt 2 tablespoons butter in a large saucepan and add the spinach. Cover the pot and simmer for about 15 minutes or until the spinach becomes limp.

In a small saucepan melt the 3 tablespoons butter and blend in the flour. Stir and cook for 2 minutes without coloring the flour. Whisk in 1 cup hot milk. Season with salt and pepper and simmer until thickened. Pour the cream sauce into the spinach and blend together and simmer for 2 minutes more or until all is well thickened. Adjust seasoning. Serves 6.

2 ten-ounce bags fresh
    spinach
2 tablespoons butter
3 tablespoons flour
1 cup hot milk
2 teaspoons salt
1 teaspoon pepper

VARIATIONS:

Almost any vegetable around can be creamed. The richness of the sauce gives vegetables a more developed combination of tastes.

NOTE:

Creamed vegetables are an excellent preparation provided that the flour in the sauce is properly cooked. Otherwise you will get a pasty, unpleasant taste.

DIRTY RICE

This rice dish gets its name from its appearance after all the ingredients are added. Since it requires the poultry gizzard, liver and heart it is usually served with birds.

Gizzard, liver, and heart
        from a whole chicken
        or duck
½ stick butter
1 chopped onion
2 toes minced garlic
4 cups chicken stock
½ teaspoon pepper
2 bay leaves
2 tablespoons minced
        parsley
¼ teaspoon thyme
2 cups rice

Chop the gizzard, liver, and heart from a chicken and sauté in the butter with the chopped onion and garlic until lightly browned. Add chicken stock, pepper, bay leaves, chopped parsley, and thyme and bring to a boil. Add the rice and simmer for 20 minutes or until the rice is tender and the chicken stock is absorbed. Adjust seasoning if necessary. Serves 6 to 8.

VARIATIONS:

Chopped pecans can be added for additional flavor.

FRIED EGGPLANT

Fried eggplant is an excellent alternate to fried potatoes. They also do quite nicely as hors d'oeuvres with cocktails before dinner. Galatoire's Restaurant has a particularly good version of these that are served to snack on while you are waiting for your dinner.

Peel the eggplants and cut them into ½- by ½-inch strips as you would potatoes. Blend the salt, pepper and cayenne with the flour. Dredge the eggplant strips in the flour, dip into the milk, and roll in the bread crumbs. Set aside.

    Heat enough oil to give you ½-inch depth in the skillet to 375 degrees. Fry the eggplants until golden on all sides. Drain on paper and serve. Serves 6.

3 medium eggplants
2 tablespoons salt
2 teaspoons black pepper
1 teaspoon cayenne
1½ cups flour
1 cup milk
1½ cups bread crumbs

VARIATIONS:

Grated Parmesan or Romano cheese added to the bread crumbs gived the fried eggplants an excellent Italian taste. Serve the fried eggplants with plenty of lemon wedges.

NOTE:

Serve them hot. Fried eggplants lose a lot of their appeal when they get cold.

    The Creoles traditionally served the fried eggplant with a small dish of powdered sugar in which to dip them.

MAQUE CHOUX

This is a dish that both the Cajuns and the Creoles have claimed to be theirs. I have seldom seen this dish in a restaurant, yet it is not uncommon to find it on the tables of both urban and rural Louisiana dwellers.

As best as I can find in my research, this dish is one that was in fact given to the Cajuns by the Indians of Louisiana, the Choctaws, and was originally called *mataché,* meaning spotted. It is a corn dish which is in fact spotted with the color of the tomato pieces. I believe the Cajuns, in their own patois, twisted this word into the more French sounding *maque choux.* The Cajuns brought the dish to the Creole community who quickly accepted it and as quickly forgot that it was not their own. But of course this is conjecture.

¾ cup bacon drippings, or
    1½ sticks butter
4 onions, chopped
1 bell pepper, chopped
2 tomatoes, chopped
4 cups corn, fresh, frozen,
    or canned
Salt and black pepper to
    taste

Melt the butter or bacon grease in a saucepan. Add the chopped onions and bell pepper. Sauté for a few minutes until they become limp. Add the corn and tomatoes. Season with salt and pepper, cover the pan, and simmer only long enough for the corn to be hot and cooked to your desired doneness. Serves 6 to 8.

VARIATIONS:

It is not uncommon to see this recipe with cream and a touch of sugar added.

You might add pimento in the place of the tomato. If so, use only about half the amount as the tomato.

This recipe makes a wonderful cold salad with a simple vinaigrette dressing.

NOTE:

Don't overcook the corn! You'll ruin the dish.

If the dish becomes too dry before the corn is cooked, add a little water.

Most of the recipes I have seen of this dish require the use of bacon grease. This is an important factor in getting the correct taste. I would use the bacon grease before the butter if I had it handy.

I hate peeling and seeding tomatoes when I cook at home. I rarely do it and it rarely makes a difference.

GLAZED TURNIPS

This is a good simple way to prepare turnips. They lose most of their bitterness in the cooking and gain a nice sweetness from the sugar.

6 medium turnips
1 stick butter
3 tablespoons brown sugar
½ teaspoon salt

Wash and scrape the turnips. Cut them into ½-inch cubes. Melt the butter with the brown sugar. Add the turnips and ½ teaspoon salt and cook covered on a low heat until the turnips are tender. Stir them around several times while cooking. Remove the cover from the pan and cook off most remaining liquid. Serves 6.

VARIATIONS:

A touch of garlic or chopped green onions would add nicely to this dish.

NOTE:

Turnips have not always been my favorite dish. It has taken my sense of taste to mature to like vegetables like turnips or belgian endive, both of which have a bitterness to them. I now count them as among my favorites.

PETITS POIS À LA FRANÇAISE

Peas have always been fun, not only because they taste good, but also because they are great to fling across the table at your sister when her head is turned. Now that we are adults we hardly ever do such things anymore, except at Thanksgiving.

I have always liked to mix up the peas on my plate with the mashed potatoes and plenty of gravy. Delicious! My favorite other preparation is Petits Pois a la Française.

Melt the butter in a saucepan and blend in the flour. Heat together while stirring until the butter and flour foam up. Add the chopped green onions, lettuce, diced ham, and bay leaf. Cook all together, stirring occasionally, until the green onions and the lettuce have wilted down completely and released all their liquid.

Add the petit pois. If the mixture is too dry, add some of the liquid from the peas. You want to achieve a smooth, yet not a watery, texture. Season with salt and pepper. Spoon into small ramekins or vegetable dishes and serve. Serves 6.

3 tablespoons butter
3 tablespoons flour
½ bunch chopped green onions
½ small head of lettuce, chopped
½ cup diced smoked ham
1 bay leaf
3 cups canned petits pois, or fresh or frozen peas (if using the canned petits pois strain and reserve the liquid)
Salt and ground white pepper to taste

VARIATIONS:

Some cooks prefer to use whole pearl onions in place of the chopped green onions. Or you could use both the pearl onions with the green onions. You could also use chopped white onions.

PLANTAINS À LA CREOLE

When I was younger it was not uncommon to find plantains on the family table. It's been years now since I have seen them in the restaurants other than the one or two Cuban eateries in the city.

In the tropics where the plantain is grown, it is cooked and eaten when it is still green. This is because the starch content of the plantain is at its richest before the fruit is ripened. The fact that we let the fruit ripen to a black state is probably a result of it being aboard ship for weeks before getting to New Orleans, at the time our cuisine was first developing.

The recipe I have begun with here is the barest and simplest preparation. From here you can take my suggestions on variations and please your own palate.

6 ripe plantains, black in
    color
2 sticks butter
1 cup brown sugar

Peel the plantains and cut them in half lengthwise. Melt the butter in a large skillet. When the butter is hot lay the plantains into the skillet. Fry them briefly on both sides to get a little color. Sprinkle the brown sugar over them and cover to simmer until they are cooked through. Serve two slices with the syrup to each person. Serves 6.

VARIATIONS:

There are many recipes for plantains but they almost all begin with the one here. Some additional ingredients that make the dish a bit more exciting are a few dashes of rum, a touch of cinnamon, a sprinkle of nutmeg, perhaps, and sometimes a dash of cayenne to give the sweetness a piquant bite. Some or even all of the above could be used together.

NOTE:

Plantains, though they very much resemble bananas, are different. First, they are not at all sweet; second, they have a taste and texture that falls somewhere between banana and squash. Even the interior color has a slight orange tinge. Their skin must be completely black before they are ripe.

SOUFFLÉE POTATOES

My great great grandfather Antoine Alciatore was the first to bring *Pommes de Terre Soufflée* or Soufflée Potatoes to this country.

The story that has been passed down for five generations in our family is the following:

During the reign of Louis Philippe, King of France, 1830 to 1848, there was a great amount of industrialization taking place in that country. One aspect of that industrialization was the expansion of the railroad system across France. One leg of this system was the newly completed run from Paris to the neighboring St. Germaine-en-Laye.

The tracks had just been completed and there was to be a great celebration for the opening of the new line. King Louis Philippe was to ride the first run of the train from Paris to St. Germain-en-Laye and there was to be a great feast on his arrival.

The great chef Collinet was presiding over the banquet preparations and had stationed a messenger at the depot to run and tell him when the train was in sight so that he could begin his final preparations. The train came into view and the messenger ran to inform Collinet as he was instructed. Into the oil went the sliced potatoes that accompanied every meal served the king.

But the king was not on the train! At the last minute his advisors had refused to let him board the train and had him ride in a carriage alongside the train to its destination.

Collinet had to remove the potatoes from the oil and let them sit until the king's actual arrival.

Some time passed and the king did finally arrive at the banquet hall and the feast was again begun. Back into the oil went the potatoes. The oil had by this time reached a high temperature from sitting on the fire and the pre-cooked potatoes did an amazing thing: they blew up like balloons.

Collinet was horrified that the potatoes were so irregular but was forced to serve them.

Louis Philippe was delighted with this new invention of Collinet's and had him come out into the banquet hall to be praised for such a novel and innovative presentation.

During the 1830s, when Antoine Alciatore was quite young he was apprenticed to the Chef Collinet at the Hotel de Noailles in Marseilles, France. It was during that apprenticeship that Collinet taught him the secret of Soufflée Potatoes. Antoine brought that recipe with him when he came to New Orleans and the Restaurant Antoine has served them ever since.

My fellow restaurateur, and student of Creole Cookery, Dr. Lawrence Hill reminds me that as another coincidence, King Louis Philippe was the only king of France that ever actually set foot in New Orleans. Of course, it was before he was king and still just the young prince traveling.

Wash and peel the potatoes. Cut them lengthwise into slices 1¼-inches wide and ⅛-inch thick. Hold them in cold water. Heat two deep fat fryers, one at 375 degrees and the other at 425 degrees. You should use an oil reccommended for frying and not for salads. Do not let the temperatures exceed those given to avoid the possibility of fire. Dry the potatoes and put a batch into the first fryer at 375 degrees. Cook the slices in small batches so you don't have too much fluctuation of temperatures in the deep fat. Let them puff and color a bit. Remove the partially cooked potatoes from the first oil and put them in the second at 425 degrees. Let them finish puffing and browning. Remove, drain on paper, salt and serve on a platter lined with paper doilies for absorbtion of excess grease. Serves 6.

4 large ripe Idaho potatoes
2 deep fat fryers and oil
Salt

NOTE:

Great care should be taken when using this recipe. Do not let this grease drip down the side of the pot or it will catch fire. Use a pot with a cover that you can use to smother the fire if it does happen to catch.

STEWED OKRA AND TOMATOES

Hibiscus esculentus, or okra, or gumbo, is originated in the tropics of the Eastern Hemisphere and is now widely cultivated in the tropics and subtropics of the Western Hemisphere. It early on became very popular in Louisiana and has become a principle vegetable in our cookery.

½ stick butter
1 large onion
1 quart okra, stems
    removed and sliced
    crosswise into ½-inch
    pieces
2 large tomatoes, chopped
2 toes garlic, minced
¼ teaspoon thyme
2 bay leaves
2 tablespoons vinegar
1 cup chicken bouillon
1½ teaspoon salt,
    or to taste
1 teaspoon pepper,
    or to taste
½ teaspoon cayenne,
    or to taste

Melt the butter in a large heavy saucepan and add the onions and okra. Sauté together for a few minutes until the onions are transparent. Add all remaining ingredients. Season with salt, pepper and cayenne. Simmer slowly for 30 minutes, or until the vegetables have achieved a stew consistency and most of the liquid is cooked out. Serves 6 to 8.

VARIATIONS:

Corn added to this or in place of the tomatoes is a good combination.

WILD AND WHITE RICE
WITH RAISINS AND PECANS

Wild rice is somewhat difficult to come by these days so we mix it with white rice to make it go farther. The combination of the two rices, along with the flavors and textures of the raisins and pecans, makes a delightful accompaniment to most entrées, especially duck and chicken.

Bring the water to a boil. Add 1½ tablespoons salt and 2 tablespoons butter and 1 cup wild rice. Cover and simmer slowly for 15 minutes. Add the white rice, raisins and pecan pieces. Cover and simmer slowly for 20 minutes more. Serves 6 to 8.	6½ cups water 1½ tablespoons salt 2 tablespoons butter 1 cup wild rice 2 cups white rice ½ cup raisins ½ cup chopped pecan pieces

VARIATIONS:

This recipe is wonderful with all wild rice. You might prefer walnuts in place of the pecans.

NOTE:

Sauté the pecans in butter to brown them and give them a nuttier taste and add them just before serving so they are crunchy.

TURNIPS AND GREENS WITH PICKLED PORK

Turnips and their greens have always been popular with the Creoles. The use of pickled pork as a seasoning meat is common practice and is done with many vegetable and bean dishes.

½ pound pickled pork
½ stick butter
1 bunch green onions, chopped
1 bunch turnips with their greens
1 cup chicken stock
1 teaspoon pepper, or to taste
1 teaspoon salt or to taste

Prepare the turnips and greens:

Cut the turnips from the greens, brush them clean under running water and cut them into ½-inch cubes. Break off the tough bottom stems from the greens and discard. Chop up the greens. Wash the chopped greens in a bowl of cool water several times. It is most important to be sure that all the hidden grit is removed from the greens before you add them to the pot. Remove from the water and set aside.

Cut the pickled pork into 1-inch cubes and sauté in a large saucepan with the butter, onions, and cubed turnips. Sauté until the turnips are cooked but not mushy and then add the turnip greens. Add 1 cup chicken stock, season with salt and pepper. Cover and simmer for 25 minutes or until all is tender. Serves 6.

VARIATIONS:

Salt pork, ham or bacon can be used in place of the pickled pork.

NOTE:

You might prefer to blanche the pickled pork in plain water to eliminate the strong taste.

Desserts

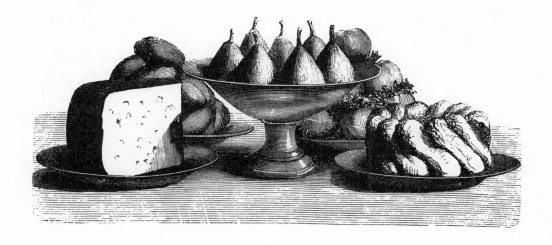

SPICED PECANS

Spiced pecans usually appear on the buffet table at Thanksgiving and Christmas. They are a nice touch to round out the menu.

Mix the sugar, salt, cinnamon, cloves, and allspice together. Put the mixture in a heavy skillet with the pecans. Cook on a medium heat, stirring constantly, until the sugar is dissolved and the pecans are completely coated with the syrup. Spoon the pecans onto waxed paper and let them cool slightly. Separate the pecans and cool completely. Makes 1 cup.

¼ cup brown sugar
½ teaspoon salt
1 teaspoon cinnamon
½ teaspoon ground cloves
½ teaspoon ground allspice
1 cup shelled pecan halves

VARIATIONS:

You can use regular sugar in place of the brown sugar. This recipe works well with walnuts.

NOTE:

This is a nice little tidbit to have on the table at coffee time.

BANANAS FOSTER

One of the great desserts to come out of the New Orleans restaurants is bananas foster from Brennan's. This is one of a group of dishes that I refer to as Haute Creole. These are dishes that have brought Creole cookery to its most sophisticated and elegant form. Bananas foster has become a standard of the restaurants here and well should it be. It is simple and delicious.

The dish was named after Richard Foster, a friend of the founding family members of Brennan's Restaurant.

6 tablespoons salted butter
1½ cups brown sugar
1 teaspoon cinnamon
6 peeled bananas, sliced
    lengthwise then
    crosswise
¼ cup banana liqueur
½ cup dark rum
6 scoops vanilla ice cream

Place the butter in a large chafing dish over a sterno flame at the table, or in a large sauté pan on the stove. Heat until it is completely melted and add the brown sugar and cinnamon. Stir until the sugar is completely melted. Add the sliced bananas. Sauté the bananas until they become slightly soft and begin to brown. Add the banana liqueur and the rum, but do not stir into the sauce. Let the liquor sit on top and heat. When hot, carefully ignite with a match. Spoon the flaming sauce over the bananas until the flame goes out. Place a scoop of ice cream on each dessert dish. Spoon 4 pieces of banana and some of the sauce over each dish of ice cream. Serve immediately. Serves 6.

VARIATIONS:

So maybe you are a hardcore chocolate ice cream lover, or only buy the most expensive boutique ice creams on the market. Use your favorite! I have no doubt you will be pleased.

NOTE:

If you don't have a pan large enough to accommodate all the bananas at one time, simply split the recipe and do it twice. It only takes minutes to do.

The bananas must be firm to start, or you will end up with a mush instead of nicely cooked pieces.

In the restaurants, this dish is prepared *à table,* with the use of a chafing dish. This is very elegant and exciting if you have the equipment. Personally, at home I prefer simplicity and do the entire cooking and flaming process in the kitchen at the stove.

BREAD PUDDING
WITH WHISKEY SAUCE

Never even the smallest crust of stale bread is wasted in the true Creole or Cajun kitchens. All is used and used in a fashion that makes the finished dish a true culinary delight. No stale bread is lost. From bread crumbs to lost bread to croutons to bread pudding—all good usages of an otherwise useless product.

Bread pudding is a treat for everyone and so simple to make. The extra ingredients that you might add on your own are what will make your version special.

2 whole eggs
2 cups milk
1 tablespoon vanilla extract
½ cup raisins
6 ounces stale french bread, about ½ standard (32-inch) loaf
1 stick butter
1 cup sugar
⅓ cup bourbon whiskey

In a bowl mix the eggs, milk, sugar, vanilla, and raisins. Break the stale bread into small pieces and add it to the mixture. Fold all together and let it soak for a few minutes. Butter a loaf pan or baking dish. Pour the entire mixture into the buttered pan and bake in a 350-degree oven for 1 hour and 15 minutes or until a knife inserted into the center of the bread pudding comes out clean.

Make the whiskey sauce:

Melt the butter and sugar together in a saucepan. Remove from the heat and pour in the bourbon. To serve, spoon the hot bread pudding onto dessert plates and spoon over some whiskey sauce. Serves 6 to 8.

VARIATIONS:

Fruit cocktail is often added to the pudding before baking to give more variety. Pecans give it a nice touch also. Almost any fruit of your choice can be added to the pudding.

The sauce is sometimes made of rum or brandy instead of bourbon.

NOTE:

I have often frozen and reheated bread pudding with great success.

CARAMEL CUSTARD

When I was eight years old our family moved to a grand new home in the uptown section of New Orleans, the University area, so called because of the several universities located within blocks of each other.

Across the street from us was a woman we got to know immediately. She had been friends with my grandmother from schoolgirl days. At the time we arrived our friend was about seventy years of age. She was tall and lithe with jet-black hair that gave her the appearance of a much younger woman.

I was idly exploring the neighborhood one hot afternoon that August of our first summer there when she caught sight of me from down the block. "Young Roy! I just finished a batch of my famous caramel custards and I need someone to test them for me." I walked over and she leaned down and kissed me hello.

"It's so hot I think we might go inside and have a glass of mint tea before we test that custard."

We went into the dark coolness of her home, through the contrasting brightness of the pristine kitchen. The appliances were old and lovely as were the glass doors, wooden cabinets and the antique copper pots and utensils and china. She sat me at the white wooden table and began her preparation of the tea. She grew mint in her garden and took a few sprigs out of the refrigerator.

"The only way to get the best taste out of the mint is to crush it. If you chop it or you boil it, you don't get the real minty taste."

She certainly seemed to know what she was talking about. She put a few leaves of the mint into a mortar and opened a jar where she kept the sugar. There was a long black stick in the sugar. I was amazed to see a stick in her sugar and asked her what it was.

"Oh, that. That's a vanilla bean. I always keep a vanilla bean in the sugar jar. It makes the sugar smell like perfume and the vanilla makes everything taste better." She passed the sugar jar under my nose and the perfume of the vanilla was exquisite. It reminded me of cake. She then made us our ice teas which were about the most refreshing drink I had ever had.

The kitchen already smelled like vanilla and sweet cream and spice.

"Now let's see about those custards." She got up from the table and walked over to the counter where there was a tray of small cups filled with an amber-colored custard. "I like to let my custards rest a while on the counter before I put them in the refrigerator. I believe it makes them taste better. Now pick one out, Roy. And pick one out for me, too."

I slowly cut my spoon into the crusty top of the custard and withdrew a bite. I tasted the spoonful. It was delicious. I had had custards many times before, but this was truly better than any. The texture was like silk on the tongue and the sweetness of the vanilla and spices came together in a manner simply heavenly.

"What's this brown stuff on the bottom?" I asked.

"That's caramelized sugar. That's why we call it Caramel Custard."

Well, I do believe I ate two or three before I left that afternoon as she told me wonderful stories of what it was like in New Orleans when she was a girl, many years ago. That afternoon we became fast friends and we would visit together often in her kitchen exchanging stories over iced mint tea and custard.

Melt the ½ cup sugar in a small heavy saucepan with the water. Bring to a boil and continue boiling until the sugar syrup has turned a caramel color. Pour it immediately into the bottom of 6 custard cups or small soufflée dishes. Let cool. In a bowl combine the eggs, the remaining sugar, the vanilla, salt and scalded milk. Beat until the sugar is dissolved. Pour the mixture into the custard cups and bake in a preheated 325-degree oven for 45 minutes or until a knife inserted into the middle of a custard comes out clean. Chill in the refrigerator before serving.

These custards can be served in the cups or turned out onto dessert dishes. Serves 6.

½ cup sugar
2 tablespoons water
4 whole eggs
½ cup sugar
1 teaspoon vanilla extract
¼ teaspoon salt
3 cups scalded milk

VARIATIONS:

A dash of cinnamon or a few drops of almond extract give this dessert a nice taste.

NOTE:

I prefer to eat the custard out of the cup with the caramelized syrup at the bottom, rather than turning the custard out onto a dish. This is where the name *crème renversée* or to turn over, comes from.

CALAS (RICE CAKES)

Calas are one of those legendary dishes in Creole cookery that one often hears about but seldom finds. They are one of those foods that years ago were sold on the streets and at the market by the old Negro women who would cook them at home and wrap them up in baskets and sell them to the passersby. They are a wonderful change from pancakes and cereals for breakfast and make a good alternate to bread at a meal.

Cook the rice.

Bring 2 cups water to a boil with 1 teaspoon salt and 1 tablespoon butter. Add 1 cup rice, cover and simmer for 20 minutes or until the rice is completely cooked and all of the liquid is absorbed.

Make the dough:

Blend the cooked rice together with the sugar, salt, and nutmeg. Dissolve the baking powder in boiling water and blend it into the mixture. Now work in the eggs and the flour 1 cup at a time. Divide the mixture into 12 flat round cakes. Fry in 2 inches of oil heated to 350 degrees until the calas are browned on both sides, about 5 minutes. Drain on paper. Dust the calas with powdered sugar and serve. Serves 6.

VARIATIONS:

You might want to serve the calas as breakfast with thick cane syrup poured over or with some good Louisiana strawberry preserves.

NOTE:

Be sure that they are cooked all the way through and are hot when served.

1 cup rice
½ cup sugar
½ teaspoon salt
½ teaspoon nutmeg
1½ teaspoon baking
    powder
1 tablespoon boiling water
3 eggs
1½ cups flour
Oil, enough to get a depth
    of 2 inches in the
    frying pan
Powdered sugar

CHERRIES JUBILEE

Cherries jubilee is a marvelous way to finish a good dinner with flair. It is really so easy and exciting to do that you will probably want to do it often.

It is a perfect celebratory dish.

1 qt. vanilla ice cream
1½ cups brandy
½ cup sugar
2 pints fresh cherries,
    pitted

Scoop the ice cream into dessert cups and put in the freezer to hold. Remove the bowls from the freezer just before preparing the cherries.

Prepare the cherries:

Heat the brandy and sugar together in a saucepan until the sugar is dissolved. Add the pitted cherries and light the liquid with a match. Spoon the cherries around in the flaming brandy until the fire goes out. Spoon the cherries with the liquid over the ice cream in the bowls. Serves 6.

VARIATIONS:

Most restaurants use canned bing cherries for this dessert. They do have good flavor and are packed in their own sweet syrup which ensures a consistent taste and availability.

Jubilee can be made with any available berry and with cut fruit such as apples and pears.

NOTE:

The brandy must be warm to ignite.

If you use canned fruit be sure not to use too much of the juice or it will water down the brandy and you will not be able to ignite it at all.

When you are warming the brandy before adding the cherries, be careful that it does not touch the fire or ignite before you want to.

PAIN PERDU (LOST BREAD)

Little of anything was ever discarded in the Creole kitchen that could not somehow be used again. Stale bread is a primary example of this. From bread crumbs to croutons to bread pudding and lost bread, there was a use for the stale french bread that was so often available. Since French bread is baked daily and becomes stale in a matter of hours there developed a preponderance of dishes dealing with the use of the stale bread. Lost bread is the root of these dishes.

In this typical offering we see the transformation of a possibly useless product, the stale bread, made into a delicious sweet dish, not unlike French toast.

Thrift was essential in the Creole kitchen, with pain perdu as perfect example. This dish is most often served for breakfast.

Beat the eggs together with the sugar until the sugar is dissolved. Blend in the vanilla extract, cinnamon and nutmeg. Whisk in the milk. Cut the french bread crosswise into 1¼ inch slices. Melt the butter in a skillet. When butter is hot, begin cooking the bread by first dipping the slices into the egg and milk mixture and then lay the slices into the hot butter. Brown the bread on both sides and remove to a serving platter. Dust the pain perdu with powdered sugar and dribble a little syrup over each slice. Serve 3 or 4 slices per person. Serves 6.

3 eggs
¼ cup sugar
1 tablespoon vanilla extract
1 tablespoon cinnamon
½ tablespoon nutmeg
1 cup milk
2 sticks butter
1 loaf stale French bread
Powdered sugar
Louisiana cane syrup

VARIATIONS:

Your favorite syrup or maybe those homemade preserves on the shelf in your refrigerator would go well here with your pain perdu.

You can make this with any bread that is not too highly flavored with herbs or garlic or onions.

NOTE:

I think the Louisiana cane syrup is important here. Steen's syrup, manufactured in Abbeville, Louisiana, will always be my favorite.

PECAN PIE

Since pecan growing is one of Louisiana's oldest industries, it is only natural that pecan pie is one of our oldest and most important desserts. And pecans combined with our dark cane syrup produce an irresistible taste. The thick, sweet, sticky filling seems somehow a most natural part of living in this exotic land.

When the family moved uptown the first few days of moving in my father would take us out to dinner at some neighborhood restaurant each night to give mother a break from the long days of unpacking and ensconcing the family into our new residence. One of those restaurants was Camelia Grill. This is New Orlean's oldest, and one of the few remaining true grills. There were two dishes that I would order there that have become my meal whenever I get the opportunity to visit. One was an unusual sandwich called a Cannibal Burger, which is basically a Steak Tartar on a bun, and the other is pecan pie. It's one of the best pecan pies I have ever tasted, home baked and absolutely delicious.

It is more than likely that the first restaurant in New Orleans to serve pecan pie was the famous Begué's. This was a restaurant in the French Market that catered to the market workers and butchers, and, eventually, gained such acclaim that all cognoscenti visiting the city would search it out. When Hypolite Begué died in 1917, the restaurant closed. The neighboring restaurant, Tujague's, is, in a way, the child of Begué's, and still serves many of the dishes that made Begué's famous. Pecan pie is one of these.

We have many things in New Orleans that we take for granted, or accept as common. For example, we have miniature pecan pies in the candy machines. You probably won't find this anywhere else. And it is one of the principle products of the bakeries of Louisiana.

Pie crust preparation:

Preheat the oven to 400 degrees. In a bowl or on a pastry board, mix together the flour, sugar, and salt. Break the butter into small pieces and blend it into the flour. The mixture should become crumbly. Work quickly on a cool surface so that the butter does not melt. Add the cold water and work in to bind the dough. If the dough becomes too soft, let it chill in the refrigerator covered with a damp cloth for a few minutes. Place the dough on a lightly floured surface and roll it out with a lightly floured rolling pin. The dough should extend 2 inches beyond the 9-inch pan. Fit the dough into the pan and crimp the edges.

Pie preparation:

In a mixing bowl, beat the eggs and blend in the sugar. Work in the syrup, vanilla, bourbon, salt, and melted butter. Add the pecans and pour the mixture into the pie crust. Bake the pie at 400 degrees for 10 minutes. Lower the temperature to 350 degrees and bake for 30 minutes more, or until the filling is set and the crust is browned. Let cool to room temperature. Serves 6 to 8.

VARIATIONS:

Use a frozen crust if you don't feel like making the pastry. It will suffice and the recipe becomes far simpler.

NOTE:

This will always be one of my favorite desserts in Louisiana cookery.

PIE CRUST INGREDIENTS:
1 cup all purpose flour
1 tablespoon sugar
½ teaspoon salt
¾ stick butter
    (6 tablespoons)
2 tablespoons cold water

PIE FILLING INGREDIENTS:
3 large eggs
1 cup brown sugar
⅔ cup dark corn syrup
½ teaspoon vanilla
3 tablespoons bourbon,
    rum, or brandy
¼ teaspoon salt
2 tablespoons melted butter
1½ cups shelled pecans

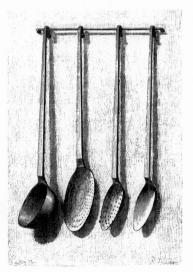

OREILLES DE COCHON (PIGS' EARS)

An old Cajun recipe, these pastries get their name from the shape they take on in cooking when the flattened dough is twisted with the fork and shaped like its namesake.

They are a real country sort of dessert and rarely, if ever, sold commercially.

½ stick butter
½ teaspoon salt
1 teaspoon baking powder
2 eggs
2 cups flour
Frying oil, enough for
     1½-inch depth in
     the skillet
½ cup sugar
1½ cups Louisiana cane
     syrup
⅛ teaspoon salt
1 cup chopped pecans

Make the pastry:

Cream the butter together with the salt, baking powder and eggs. Work in the flour 1 cup at a time. Knead the dough on a floured surface for a few minutes. Divide the dough into 12 pieces and roll the pieces into balls. Roll each ball out into a ⅛-inch thick circle. Put enough oil in a heavy skillet to get a depth of 1½ inches. Heat the oil to 375 degrees. Cook the Pigs' Ears one at a time. Put one round of dough into the oil and as soon as it floats to the top jab the center with a long fork and give it a twist to give the pastry the shape of pigs' ears. Fry on both sides briefly until done and place them on paper to drain. When the 12 pieces are all done make your topping:

Make the topping:

Put the sugar, syrup, pinch salt, and chopped pecans in a heavy saucepan and bring to a boil. Continue boiling until the syrup has reached the soft ball stage when dropped in a glass of cold water. Dribble the syrup and pecans over the pastry until all is used. Makes 12 Pigs' Ears. Serves 6 or 12.

VARIATIONS:

There isn't any variance if you are going to have the real thing.

NOTE:

The Pigs' Ears should be served hot out of the pot when they are their best.

PRALINES

This is the most famous confection of the Creoles. Although there are many variations available the true praline is made with pecans and the sugar is cooked to the hard crack stage. This makes the praline sort of crumbly when you bite into it.

Simplicity is the key here; simple and delicious.

1½ cup white sugar
1½ cups brown sugar
¼ teaspoon salt
1 cup milk
2 tablespoons butter
1 teaspoon vanilla extract
2 cups pecan meat
Buttered wax paper
    or foil.

Combine the white sugar, brown sugar, salt, and milk in a heavy saucepan and bring to a boil. Cook at a low boil, stirring constantly, until a drop of the syrup in cold water forms a hard ball. Remove from the heat and beat in the butter, vanilla extract, and pecans. Continue beating the mixture while it is cooling until it thickens and becomes creamy, about 3 minutes. Transfer the mixture, spoon by spoon, onto buttered waxed paper or foil. Be sure to get some pecan pieces into each praline. Let cool and serve. These may be stored in a covered container. Makes about 2 dozen pralines.

VARIATIONS:

Pralines can be made "chewy" by not cooking the sugar syrup as long, only to "soft ball" stage. Other flavors can be added for variety.

NOTE:

These are nice to have around to have with coffee after dinner or as a treat for the kids.

GINGERBREAD STAGE PLANKS

When I first began working at Antoine's Restaurant over eighteen years ago, some of the old guard waiters from the country in Louisiana would bring in treats from the bakeries in their towns to have as breakfast or just snacks during the day. One of these treats was gingerbread planks. Their dark, smooth, almost skinlike texture, got them the name "mulatto's stomach." We used to like to dip them in hot, sweet café au lait.

Cream the butter and blend in the ginger and the syrup. Blend in the milk. Dissolve the soda in water and stir it into the mixture. Work in the flour 1 cup at a time. When the dough is smooth, pour it onto the greased baking sheets in 2- by 4-inch rectangles. Leave space between; they will spread during baking. This will yield about 12 planks.

   Bake in a preheated 400-degree oven for 10 minutes or until the gingerbread is cooked all the way through. Remove, cool and serve. Makes 12 planks.

1 stick butter
1 tablespoons powdered ginger
1 cup molasses syrup
1 cup milk
1 teaspoon baking soda
3 cups flour
2 greased baking sheets

VARIATIONS:

Cinnamon and nutmeg add nice additional flavors to the planks.

NOTE:

These gingerbread planks really taste like an old-fashioned recipe. They are not too sweet and are a bit spicy from the ginger.

Index